YOU CAN CHANGE  THE WORLD

LUCY BELL

Andrews McMeel
PUBLISHING®

Andrews McMeel Publishing
a division of Andrews McMeel Universal
1130 Walnut Street, Kansas City, Missouri 64106

www.andrewsmcmeel.com

First published in Australia in 2019 by Pantera Press Pty Limited
P.O. Box 1989, Neutral Bay, NSW, Australia 2089

20 21 22 23 24 SHO 10 9 8 7 6 5 4 3 2 1

ISBN: 978-1-5248-6092-9

Library of Congress Control Number: 2020938280

Cover Design and Illustrations: Astred Hicks
Internal Design: Elysia Clapin
Editor: Kevin Kotur
Art Director: Julie Barnes
Production Editor: Margaret Daniels
Production Manager: Carol Coe

Made by:
Shanghai Offset Printing Products LTD.
Plant 1, No.39 HengLing North Road, NianFeng Community,
PingDi Subdistrict, LongGang District, Shenzhen,
Guangdong Province, China 518110
1st printing—06/29/2020

For Adrian and Francesca,
who showed me how to love the planet
and all the creatures who live on it.

One child, one teacher, one book,
and one pen can change the world.
MALALA YOUSAFZAI

CONTENTS

EARTH IS AN INCREDIBLE PLANET, home to amazing creatures, plants, beaches, rivers, streams, forests, and mountains. There are so many animals in the world that we can't even count them—we can only guess! Scientists estimate that there could be anywhere from two million to fifty million different species on Earth, with thousands more being discovered every year. And we share this planet with all of them. Earth is our friend, our family, and our home.

But every day, we see problems we would like to fix. A piece of trash in a green, grassy park. Plastic water bottles buried in the sand at the beach. A garbage bin overflowing onto the street. A skinny, stray dog. A homeless person on a cold day.

We hear that the ocean is being polluted, animals are dying, and species are going extinct. That climate change is warming up the planet, melting icebergs, and threatening animals and people.

When we hear about these problems, most of us want to help, but it's hard to know where to start. And some of these problems are so big, they can seem impossible for one person to fix. But we can fix them, if we each do our part.

Human beings are some of the smartest creatures ever to walk the Earth, but we have also made some big mistakes. Now it's time for us to work together to fix those mistakes.

To do that, we have to take action. Kids are the future—you can save the world, one step at a time. As you will discover in this book, there are lots of amazing children in the world, just like you!

If you want to join the mission to save our planet, then this is the book for you.

These pages contain information, ideas, and activities to show you, your friends, and family how to make simple changes every day to make the planet a safer, happier, and greener place. Because it's up to us to protect our Earth.

Things to remember when you're changing the world:

- Changing the world won't happen in a day, and you don't have to do everything at once. It's all about making a few changes at a time.
- Start with the things that are easiest for you. You don't need to read this book in order—pick the activities you want to do most.
- This book is about being more aware of the things you are doing and the choices you are making every day. It's not always possible to make the best choice, but it's important to be informed, so you know how your actions affect the world around you.
- Saving the planet is fun! We're all on our own journey, and every day we can do something to help the fight.
- Track your progress so you can see all the important changes you have made. Everything you do matters.

PLASTIC

THE NUMBER OF plastic items on Earth is in the trillions. It is estimated that there are more than five trillion pieces of plastic in the ocean alone. That is a huge number! With five trillion teaspoons of water, you could fill over 9,800 Olympic swimming pools. And if you joined all of those pieces of plastic together, they would go around the whole planet more than 4,000 times.

Plastic never goes away. In fact, every piece of plastic ever made still exists on Earth in some form.

Plastic objects break down into smaller microplastics, but they never disappear completely. Plastic contains chemicals that are harmful to humans, and animals often mistake small bits of plastic for food and feed them to their young, who can choke on them or become sick. It piles up in our environment, and it's showing no signs of slowing down.

Getting rid of the plastic in our lives is almost impossible. How many things in your house are made of plastic or have plastic parts? Maybe too many to count!

But cutting back a little bit can make a big difference. Every time you choose an alternative to plastic, you're helping save an animal, save our oceans, and stop the spread of toxic chemicals, making the world a happier place.

And there's an easy way for you to start: with single-use plastics. Single-use plastics are objects made of plastic, such as straws, that you only use once before throwing them away. Lots of countries are trying to ban single-use plastics, but for now, we can do our best to avoid them.

WATER

BOTTLES

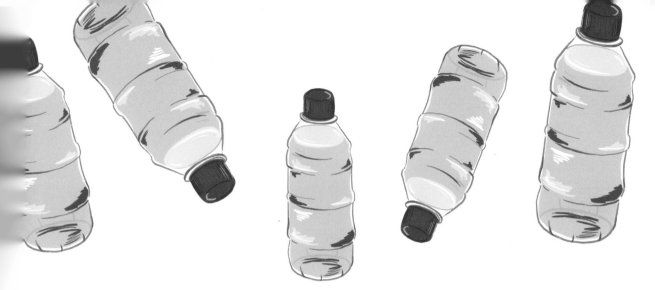

IT'S STRANGE JUST how many bottles of water we buy each year, even though we have access to clean tap water.

Bottled water first came to America in the 1970s. At the time, no one actually believed people would pay for bottled water when they could get it for free. But incredibly, they did! Now, each year, Americans buy about 700,000 tons of plastic drink bottles, yet we recycle fewer than one in four of those bottles. We can do better than that!

Instead of buying your water in a plastic bottle, get a reusable water bottle, such as a stainless-steel bottle. These are available in a range of colors, sizes, and patterns and will last you a long time. Alternatively, you can start by reusing bottles you already own.

Every minute, more than a million bottles of water are bought worldwide.

FACT	Every year, around thirty-eight billion plastic water bottles end up in landfills in the United States alone.

EARTH BOTTLES

Danni Carr is a musician and mother of two who started a business called Earth Bottles in 2014 to help try to stop the rising plastic issue in its tracks.

Driven by a passion to do something about the single-use plastics that had begun to pile up in her environment, Danni and her husband, musician Ash Grunwald, work together to encourage people to eradicate plastic from their lives, also partnering with the Clean Coast Collection to fund beach cleanups around the world.

Along with their faux-timber drink bottles, Earth Bottles now have stainless steel straws, coffee cups, thermoses, and shopping bags.

What are your top tips for kids who want to quit plastic?

1. Ask Mom and Dad to make your school lunches plastic-free. They can use a reusable lunchbox, beeswax wraps if anything needs wrapping, and lots of fresh yummy food. Always pack your reusable water bottle.

2. Try having a plastic-free birthday party! You could use bubbles instead of balloons, plastic-free party bags, and cook some easy recipes with Mom and Dad for treats rather than buying food packaged in plastic. Ask your friends to bring plastic-free gifts.

3. Remind Mom and Dad every time you go out to pack your reusable bottles and straws and to pack your snacks into a reusable lunchbox.

4. Choose plastic-free toys. Things like books, board games, wooden toys or balls, and outdoorsy things are great options instead of toys made from, and packaged in, heaps of plastic.

TIP

You can also buy reusable milkshake and juice cups, which you can take to cafes or fill with your own homemade drinks.

COFFEE CUPS

NEXT TIME YOU'RE OUT, take a look at all the people drinking out of takeaway coffee cups—they're everywhere!

You've probably seen the plastic lids lying all over the place, squashed on the side of the road or the sidewalk. Often these lids actually CAN be recycled, so if you're using a takeaway cup, make sure you separate the lid from the cup before throwing them both away.

> To-go coffee cups are a huge contributor to the problem of single-use plastics. The cups are usually made of either paper coated with plastic or Styrofoam, neither of which can be recycled.

If you buy a lot of hot drinks, like hot chocolate, tea, or coffee, or you know anyone who does, think about getting a reusable cup, like a KeepCup, as a way of cutting down on plastic. Some cafes even offer discounts if you bring your own cup. Better still, spread the word among cafes, pointing out the benefits to our Earth if they can encourage their customers to use more planet-friendly alternatives. In Australia, for example, some cafes are now registering with an organization called Responsible Cafes to learn to reduce their ecological footprint and also educate their customers. Start talking to your local cafes and inspire them to make a difference today.

FACT	Worldwide, people use over sixteen billion to-go coffee cups every year.

STRAWS

AMERICANS use hundreds of millions of straws every day. Each of these straws takes more than two hundred years to break down. That means the straws you use today will still be around when your great-great-great-great-great-grandchildren are alive.

So next time you get a drink or a milkshake at the canteen or a cafe or restaurant, just ask for no straw.

If you really want to keep using straws, here are some things you could try instead. Just remember to take them with you:

- Metal straws, which you can clean and reuse.
- Bamboo straws, which are also reusable.
- Paper straws.

Many straws end up in the bellies of sea animals, which makes them very sick. Some even get stuck in turtles' noses.

FACT One hundred thousand marine creatures and around one million sea birds die each year from plastic entanglement.

MILO CRESS
United States of America

Milo Cress is the founder, co-director, and spokesperson of the Be Straw Free project. As a kid, Milo was always interested in conservation and the environment—he won an award for a solar-powered popcorn machine when he was just six years old!

But it wasn't until he moved to Vermont that Milo took an interest in plastic waste. He noticed that every time he ordered a drink at a restaurant, it came with a straw, even though he didn't need one. That made him wonder how many straws were used in America every day. When he couldn't find any information, Milo called straw manufacturers to make an estimate of his own. What he learned was astounding: between all of the cafes, restaurants, schools, hospitals, convenience stores, cafeterias, and more, Americans use 500 million straws a day!

"This planet is not a place that kids will inherit at some point, far off in the distant future. We live here right now, and share this planet already, which is why it's so important that we take individual and collective responsibility for its well-being."

So in 2011, at age nine, Milo started the Be Straw Free campaign to coordinate businesses, schools, environmental groups, and everyday citizens with one common goal: reducing the use of plastic straws. The message was simple—establishments should ask if people want a straw instead of providing one automatically, and consumers should order their drink without a straw if they don't want one.

Within no time, Be Straw Free started picking up steam, and Milo partnered with the environmental group Eco-Cycle. News outlets across the country began sharing his story. The National Park Service promoted the campaign. And Milo was asked to speak to schools, conferences, organizations, community leaders, and even the Vermont State Legislature.

More recent estimates of straw use in America are closer to 300 or 400 million per day, but that's still far too many. Thankfully, due in part to Milo's work, more and more people are turning to reusable straws—or none at all. Companies across the country are phasing out plastic straws, and entire cities like San Francisco and Seattle are also trying to make the switch. And it all began with a little curiosity and the desire to make the world a better place.

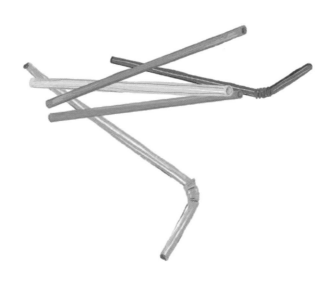

DID YOU KNOW?

There are more plastic flamingos in the world than real ones.

FOOD WRAPPING

IT'S IMPORTANT to keep food covered when you put it in the fridge. Unfortunately, the main thing we use to cover our bowls of leftover spaghetti, cheese, half-eaten chocolate bars, and sandwiches is cling wrap, which is made of—you guessed it—plastic!

Other things you can use to keep your food fresh without using plastic include:

- Beeswax wraps—these are often available at markets, or you can easily find them online.
- Reusable silicon food covers.
- Glass containers and jars.
- Stainless-steel containers.
- Fabric wraps like linen for bread and sandwiches.

TIP

You know when you order to go and they put it in a plastic container? Next time, try bringing your own container.

REUSABLE SHOPPING BAGS

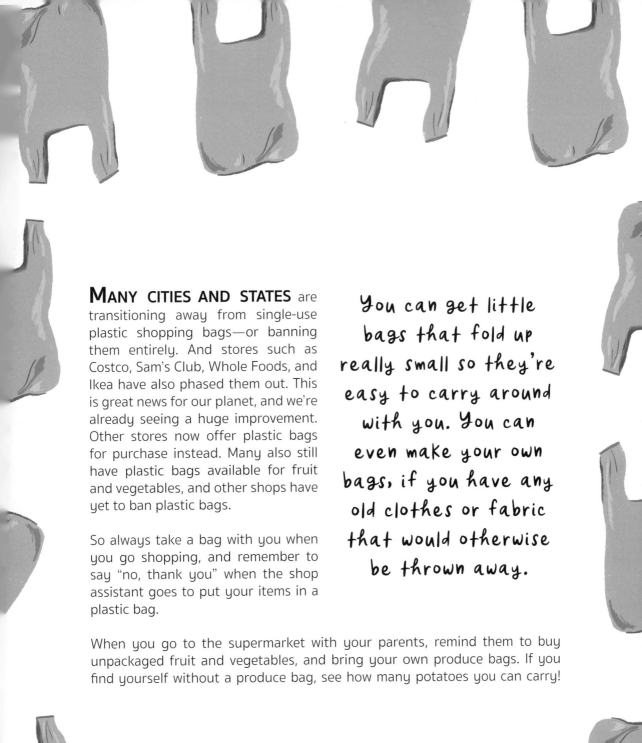

MANY CITIES AND STATES are transitioning away from single-use plastic shopping bags—or banning them entirely. And stores such as Costco, Sam's Club, Whole Foods, and Ikea have also phased them out. This is great news for our planet, and we're already seeing a huge improvement. Other stores now offer plastic bags for purchase instead. Many also still have plastic bags available for fruit and vegetables, and other shops have yet to ban plastic bags.

So always take a bag with you when you go shopping, and remember to say "no, thank you" when the shop assistant goes to put your items in a plastic bag.

You can get little bags that fold up really small so they're easy to carry around with you. You can even make your own bags, if you have any old clothes or fabric that would otherwise be thrown away.

When you go to the supermarket with your parents, remind them to buy unpackaged fruit and vegetables, and bring your own produce bags. If you find yourself without a produce bag, see how many potatoes you can carry!

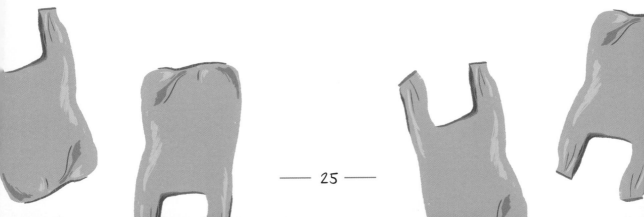

FACT

Every single known species of turtle has been found with plastic in or around its body.

TIP

Whenever you are about to buy something made of plastic, ask yourself:

- Do I actually need to buy this?
- Can I buy an alternative product that's not made of plastic?
- If I really need it, is there a way I can reuse the plastic once I'm finished with it?

AMY & ELLA MEEK

United Kingdom

Amy and Ella Meek are two sisters who decided they wanted to save the world. They are fifteen and thirteen years old, and according to them, they're just two regular kids. But they're not waiting for the adults to do the work—they think it's up to kids to take action.

Amy and Ella were born in Nottingham in England, and they are true adventurers. One year, they did a "year of adventures" challenge and were homeschooled while their family traveled around England in a trailer. They completed one hundred adventures, including canoeing down a river, sleeping in the woods, exploring a cave, and cooking on a beach. Wow! Ella says her favorite part was sleeping on a pebbly beach and seeing lots of shooting stars.

A few years ago, Amy and Ella started the organization Kids Against Plastic to teach people about the impact single-use plastics have on the environment.

Amy and Ella have visited schools, attended festivals and conferences, spoken to politicians and celebrities all over the world, done a TEDx talk, and also traveled around the UK for eXXpedition, an all-women scientific research mission that explores the ocean and collects plastic samples to raise awareness about how plastic affects our environment and health. Amy and Ella even got a personal letter from the British prime minister, Theresa May.

Amy and Ella are on a mission to pick up one hundred thousand pieces of the big four plastics—one for every sea mammal killed by plastic in the oceans each year. These big four plastic polluters are:

- Cups and lids.
- Straws.
- Bottles.
- Bags.

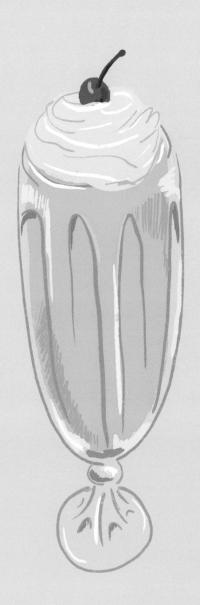

The growing use of plastic is an urgent problem, but with the work that kids like Amy and Ella are doing, there is hope. You don't have to start a campaign like they did, but you can become what they call "plastic clever" and be smart about the plastic products you use.

It might not seem like these small changes make a difference, but THEY REALLY DO! So what are you waiting for? Start getting plastic clever!

THROWING A PLASTIC-FREE PARTY

BIRTHDAY PARTIES are heaps of fun, but they can sometimes involve a lot of plastic. Try these ideas for a planet-friendly, plastic-free party. They can also make your party unique and even more special.

- Send your party invitations electronically, or send your guests a packet of seeds with a note telling them to bring the seeds to plant at your party.
- If you are having a small party, use your own plates, glasses, and cutlery, or encourage your friends to bring their own.
- Use compostable or plant-based plates and cups instead of plastic, and cutlery made out of bamboo—just check that they're from a sustainable source.
- Use repurposed jam jars for drinks instead of plastic cups.
- Use natural beeswax candles for your cake.
- Use paper instead of plastic bags for your party bags. Or, instead of party bags, give each guest a pot and some seeds to grow their very own potted plant.
- Plastic-free party activities could include tie-dyeing a T-shirt or socks, making pottery, playing hide-and-seek or musical chairs, making beeswax candles or a birdhouse, or planting the seeds you sent with your invitations. You could even go fruit picking.

Have fun and change the world at the same time!

— DECORATING —

Instead of using balloons as party decorations, try things like tissue-paper pompoms, streamers, origami, kites, tea lights, or solar fairy lights. Or use things from nature, like flowers in repurposed jars, leaves, pebbles, stones, and shells. You can also have your party outdoors, where nature is your decoration.

OTHER THINGS TO AVOID: glitter, party horns, confetti, plastic party bags, single-use plastic tablecloths and banners, and plastic plates, cups, and cutlery.

— GIFT IDEAS —

Gifts are always exciting at first, but this excitement quickly wears off. Try to choose gifts that are useful or that will last someone a long time. It's also good to avoid things that are heavily packaged in plastic. Here are some planet-friendly gift ideas:

- Books.
- Wooden toys.
- Homemade gifts, like cookies, jam, stuffed toys, a handmade pot, woodwork, bath salts, or a painting.
- Plants, seeds, and gardening tools.
- Cooking equipment and cookbooks.
- A reusable water bottle or KeepCup.
- A stainless-steel bento-style lunchbox.
- Sprout pencils—these are wooden pencils that contain seeds, which you can plant when you're done using the pencil.
- Beeswax or soy-wax crayons.
- Bamboo toothbrush.
- Sewing kit.
- Toys made from recycled plastic.
- Experiences, like movie tickets or tickets to a show, a cooking class, museum entry, a pottery-making class, music lessons, a train or ferry ride, or a day trip somewhere.
- Secondhand gifts, such as a pre-loved toy or book that's still in good condition.
- Instead of physical gifts, you can give donations to a children's hospital or a charity, or sponsor an orangutan, for example.

IN THE BATHROOM

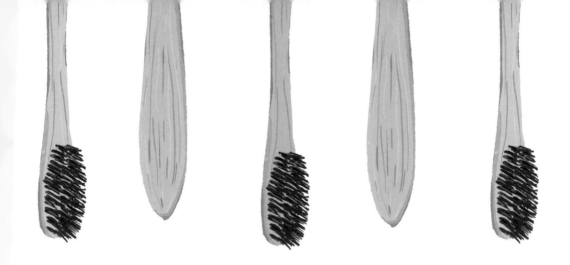

LOOK AROUND your bathroom at all the things made of plastic—toothbrushes; toothpaste tubes; dental floss; loofahs and sponges; containers for body wash, moisturizer, shampoo, conditioner, lip balm, and deodorant; combs and hairbrushes; plastic razors; cotton buds; soap packets; bath toys; maybe even a shower curtain. The list seems never-ending, doesn't it?

Start by changing just one thing at a time, and do your research—there are plastic-free alternatives to most of these products.

FACT	Toothbrushes are one of the top ten items found in coastal cleanups.

TIP

You can use coconut oil on dry lips, elbows, and knees. You can buy it in a glass jar, and you only need to use a tiny amount, so it lasts for ages!

— MICROBEADS —

Check the labels on your toothpaste, body wash, cleansers, exfoliators, sunscreen, and moisturizer to make sure the products you use don't contain microbeads. Microbeads are tiny bits of plastic that are added to a whole range of products, and they have been banned in several countries. Because microbeads are so small, they end up in our sewer system before making their way into the ocean—and they've even been found in our food!

To make sure your products don't contain these nasty bits of plastic, check the labels for the following ingredients:

- Polyethylene.
- Polypropylene.
- Polyethylene terephthalate.
- Polymethyl methacrylate.
- Polylactic acid.
- Nylon.

— BAMBOO — TOOTHBRUSHES

A bamboo toothbrush is a great alternative to a plastic one, especially if you have a compost bin so you can compost the handle.

ACTIVITY

MAKING A T-SHIRT BAG

— PERSONAL — CARE PRODUCTS

To cut down on the amount of plastic you buy, try using bar shampoo instead of shampoo in plastic bottles. You can get bar shampoo from cosmetic stores like Lush, at some local markets, or through online retailers.

You could also make your own natural hair rinses, treatments, conditioners, body wash, and other personal care products. That way, as well as rejecting plastic, you can avoid ingredients such as the following, which have been linked to a number of health hazards for people.

- Sodium lauryl sulfate (SLS).
- Sodium laureth sulfate (SLES).
- Fragrance or perfume.
- Parabens.
- Sodium chloride.
- Propylene glycol.
- Isopropyl alcohol.
- Cocamidopropyl betaine (CAPB).
- Formaldehyde.
- Triclosan.

FACT	The disposable diapers that you wore as a baby will last longer than you will.

HAIR CARE: Try the following recipes, or come up with some of your own using natural ingredients such as honey, avocado, plain yogurt, coconut oil, olive oil, rosemary, apple cider vinegar, eggs, and lemon juice.

RECIPE

BANANARAMA HAIR SMOOTHIE

This sweet conditioner will leave your hair looking sleek and shiny. Bananas contain potassium, natural oils, and vitamins, which help protect your hair. Olive oil repairs damaged hair and prevents dandruff. Honey seals moisture into your hair and also contains beneficial antioxidants. This conditioner is so natural, it's almost good enough to eat!

You'll need:

- 1 mashed banana.
- 1 tablespoon olive oil.
- 2 tablespoons honey (it's best to use local organic).

What to do: Mix all the ingredients together thoroughly until smooth, then apply evenly to damp hair. Wait for 10 to 15 minutes, then rinse well. Use once or twice a week.

APPLE CIDER HAIR RINSE

This apple cider vinegar hair rinse is full of nutrients that will help get rid of tangles and frizz. It will also get rid of the buildup left by other hair products and make your hair shine.

You'll need:

- ⅓ cup apple cider vinegar (look for ones labelled "raw", "organic," or "unfiltered," which will be cloudy and sometimes have sediment at the bottom).
- ⅔ cup water.

What to do: Mix the vinegar and water together. If your hair is oily, you might need more vinegar; if your hair is dry, you can use less vinegar. After you've wet your hair in the shower, tilt your head back to avoid getting the mixture in your eyes and pour it through your hair. Massage into your scalp, wait thirty seconds, then rinse.

RECIPE

LAVENDER BATH SALTS

For a relaxing and luxurious bath that's great for your muscles—especially if you've been doing lots of physical activities—try making your own bath salts instead of buying products that come in plastic. The Epsom salt in bath salts is made of magnesium sulfate, which is believed to relieve muscle pain and even help heal cuts.

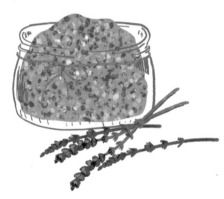

You can experiment with different types of essential oils, herbs, and dried flowers to make your salts. Bath salts also make a great gift, and you can decorate the repurposed jar!

You'll need:

- 2 cups Epsom salt.
- ¼ cup Himalayan rock salt.
- 2 tablespoons coconut oil.
- 10–15 drops lavender essential oil (available from most chemists and supermarkets).
- Optional: dried lavender, dried rosebuds, 2 tablespoons chamomile or mint tea, herbs from your garden.

What to do: Mix all the ingredients together in a large bowl, then store in a sealable glass jar, such as an old jam or honey jar. Use about ¼ cup of salts in each bath.

RECIPE

TIP

If you have any expired herbal teas, you can add them to your bath salts instead of throwing them away.

RECIPE

TOOTHPASTE

This all-natural toothpaste is great for your morning brush. If you find the taste isn't sweet enough, you can add 1 teaspoon of stevia to the mix. You can buy stevia from your local supermarket or health-food store.

You'll need:

- ⅓ cup coconut oil, slightly softened.
- 1–2 tablespoons baking soda.
- 15 drops peppermint essential oil.

What to do: Mix all the ingredients together and store in a repurposed glass jar. Simple!

— WASHCLOTHS —

Use biodegradable, natural-fiber washcloths and natural loofahs instead of plastic or nylon sponges. That way you can throw them on your compost when they get old. Some natural fibers to look for include:

- Organic bamboo.
- Coconut fibers.
- Agave.
- Hemp.

— TOILET PAPER —

Try to buy bamboo or recycled toilet paper. Also look for toilet rolls that are wrapped in paper rather than plastic. One company doing good things is Who Gives A Crap. They donate 50 percent of their profits to help build toilets for people in need.

HOW MUCH PLASTIC DO YOU USE?

For one week, write down everything you use that's made of plastic. At the end of the week, next to each item write what you could have done to avoid using it.

FACT

More than seventeen *trillion* pounds of plastic have been produced in the world.

ETHICAL AND ENVIRONMENTALLY FRIENDLY CLOTHING

IN THE OLD DAYS, if someone damaged an item of clothing or a pair of shoes, they would get them repaired. Now, we just throw them away and buy a replacement. This change in our approach has been caused by fast fashion. Fast fashion is cheap trendy clothing that's produced in huge amounts and made available to buyers as quickly as possible. Fast fashion makes it very easy to replace our clothes, but it also means the clothes we buy don't last very long, and this has a huge environmental impact. Americans throw away fourteen million tons of clothing each year, which comes out to eighty pounds per person.

Four out of ten Americans say they have put clothing in the trash rather than giving it to a friend, donating it, or repairing it.

The most important thing to remember when buying clothing is quality over quantity. In other words, it's better to spend your money on one or two more expensive items that you know are ethically made and will last you a long time (quality), rather than buying lots of cheap garments that will fall apart easily (quantity).

Buying ethical clothing is important for many reasons. Two of the main ones are:

- Clothes are made by human beings—often women and sometimes children. Many get paid hardly any money for their work. Ethical clothing brands make sure the people who produce their clothing are paid fairly and treated with respect.

- Making clothing involves the use of extremely harsh chemicals and creates millions of tons of textile waste every year. Ethical fashion aims to reduce the environmental impact of this process.

FACT

Nearly 85 percent of the textiles bought by Americans ends up in a landfill.

WHEN IT COMES TO CLOTHES, it's best to buy items made from natural materials like organic cotton, rather than synthetic fibers like polyester. If possible, try to buy from companies that produce eco-friendly, fair-trade clothing and have sustainable, ethical practices.

Look on the labels for words like:
- Organic cotton.
- Cotton (this is good, because it's a natural, breathable material from a renewable source—but it can also be bad, because lots of chemicals are used in the production of clothing).
- Bamboo.
- Hemp.
- Linen.
- Recycled polyester.
- Fair trade.
- Ethical.
- Sustainable.
- Vegan.
- Made in USA.
- Made in Canada.

Avoid clothes with labels that use words like:
- Polyester (doesn't break down and releases plastic microfibers).
- Nylon.
- Rayon.
- Spandex.
- Made in China.
- Made in Bangladesh.

GOOD ON YOU

Good On You is a group of campaigners, fashion professionals, scientists, writers, and developers who have come together to try to put an end to the problems of pollution, waste, and poorly treated workers that are the result of fast fashion. Through their analysis, Good On You scores some of the world's most popular fashion brands to make sure people know how the clothes they're buying impact the planet and its people, so they can make smarter, more ethical choices.

What are your top tips for kids who want to learn more about ethical clothing?

1. Think about if you really need something before buying it.

2. Go for vintage, thrift shop, resale apps, and clothes swaps over buying new clothing.

3. Take care of your clothes so they last longer.

4. Find out which brands do right by people, the planet, and animals by checking how they rate on the Good On You app or website.

THRIFT
SHOPS

WE ALL NEED to buy fewer items of clothing and make them last longer. But what do you do if you need new clothes or just want to go clothes shopping for fun? We all love getting new things, after all. Fortunately, it's still possible to do this and help the planet by going thrift shopping instead. Get some friends together and go bargain hunting—there are many treasures to be found in thrift shops, and you can often find quality clothing brands for a much cheaper price. And you'll probably come away with clothing that will last you a long time.

Thrift shops only sell clothing that is in good condition, and fast-fashion items often don't last long enough to be sold off secondhand!

By shopping at charity stores, as well as donating your old things to them, you're keeping these items from ending up in a landfill while also helping a good cause.

FACT

Along with oil and livestock, the fashion industry is one of the biggest polluters in the world.

FELIX & FRIEDA MONTEFIORE

Australia

Felix and Frieda are a brother and sister who live in the Blue Mountains in New South Wales. Felix runs a small business selling ethically sourced, organic cotton T-shirts, which he prints with his own hand-drawn designs. Frieda is an eco-warrior who is very worried about plastic in the environment. She does targeted cleanups around her local lakes and parks, and she gets her parents involved too!

Felix

---

1. How old are you now, and how old were you when you started making T-shirts?

I'm ten, and I started making T-shirts when I was eight.

2. What inspired you to start making T-shirts?

I grew up in a creative family and Mom was always printing, and I wanted to do some too.

3. What's your favorite pastime or hobby?

At the moment I love creating short movies with stop-motion animation.

4. Tell us about your T-shirt designs.

My grandfather is obsessed with robots and vintage toys and has a huge collection. I started drawing them for fun and thought they would make great T-shirt designs.

5. Why did you start your business?

Because I had so much fun making T-shirts and I thought I could make some money. This helped to buy more T-shirts so I could do more designs. I don't want people to be working hard and getting paid hardly anything. People should get paid properly for the work they do. It's only fair. I have also chosen organic cotton, because it's better for the waterways and the environment. It's been good, and I've also learned a little bit about how business works.

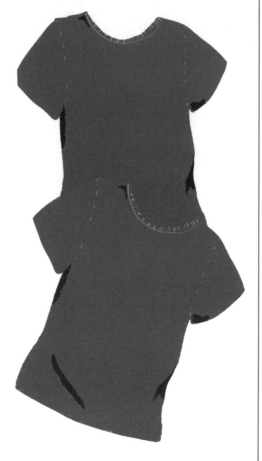

6. If you could change one thing in the world, what would it be?

I would make a campaign for everyone on Earth to pick up all the plastic and put it in a rocket and fly it into space where it could make another planet. This would reduce gravity so we could all jump higher! Seriously though, if I could change one thing, I would love to reduce the amount of plastic on Earth. Once it exists, plastic lasts forever. It's a big problem.

7. Do you have any tips for other kids who want to make a difference?

See if you can reuse something before you chuck it out.

Get your parents to recycle soft plastics. Soft plastics are one of the biggest forms of waste in our bins and they can be recycled. You just need to collect them and take them to the supermarket. Sometimes adults need reminding, but if you explain how important it is, they will get used to it.

Start a compost to recycle food scraps. It's easy. You just need a compost bin and a benchtop bin. You need to take the scraps out every day so it doesn't get smelly. Be the one to do this. Adults already have a lot going on, so if you do this, the adults will be much happier to start recycling food waste.

Frieda

1. How old are you now and how old were you when you decided that you wanted to change the world for the better?
About a year ago, when I was seven, our family watched the documentary *War on Waste* and I was very upset to see all the damage that plastic does to the creatures. There is too much of it! Way too much (angry face)!! So I started making reusable produce bags.

"When the supermarkets got rid of plastic bags, I noticed that there were still plastic bags for buying fruit, so I started to make bags that were reusable for this."

2. Where did you grow up and how did that inspire you?
I grew up in Newcastle and the Blue Mountains. These two places are so beautiful! I have been able to swim in oceans, lakes, and rivers, go for bush walks, see animals like ocean creatures with my goggles, also lyrebirds, bowerbirds, black cockatoos. I don't want plastic bags to get into waterways and hurt the creatures.

3. What's your favorite pastime or hobby?
I love snorkelling, swimming, riding my bike. I love catching bugs and lizards, looking at them and then letting them go. I would love to be allowed to have more pets!

4. If you could change one thing in the world, what would it be?
I would get rid of all the plastic in the oceans and also make an animal rescue place for all the animals that are hurt.

5. Do you have any tips for other kids who want to make a difference?
Ask your parents to get you a bucket, tongs, and gloves—and make sure they get some too. Then you can pick up trash when you see it in the bush or at the beach.

BE YOUR OWN FASHION DESIGNER

Repairing clothes is actually quite easy. Using a needle and thread, you can fix any tears or holes in your clothes and sew on new buttons. If you grow too tall for a pair of pants, you could turn them into shorts instead. Look at ways to turn your outgrown clothes into something else. You could even learn to make your own clothes!

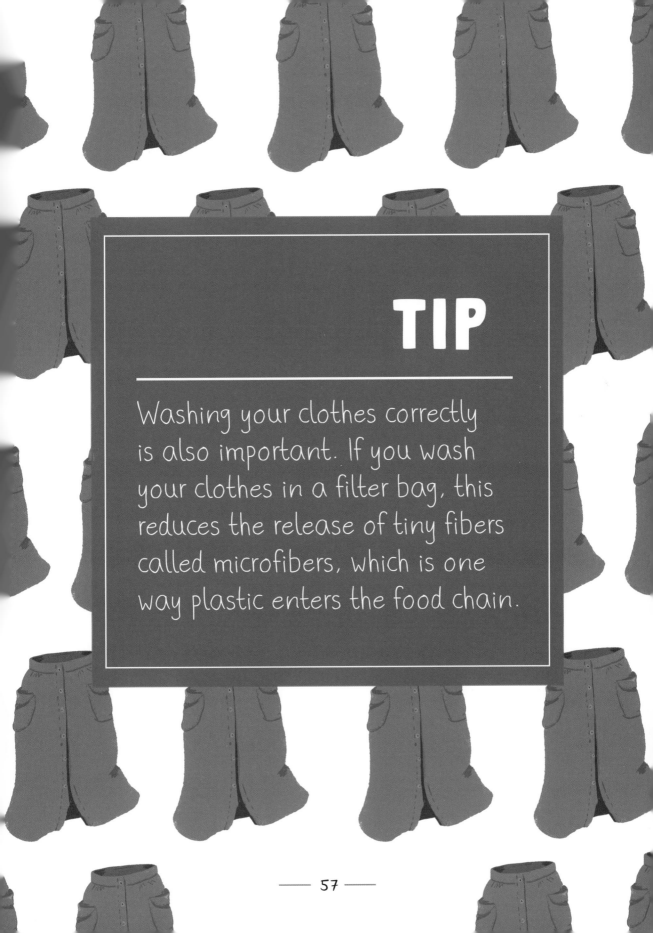

TIP

Washing your clothes correctly is also important. If you wash your clothes in a filter bag, this reduces the release of tiny fibers called microfibers, which is one way plastic enters the food chain.

MAYA PENN

United States of America

One day, Maya found a piece of fabric lying in her house. Bursting with ideas, she used that piece of fabric to make a zebra-print headband decorated with a butterfly—the Zebra-Fly. Soon she began creating all sorts of accessories. When she wore them on the street, people would give her compliments and even ask if she had any accessories for sale.

Maya donates 10–20 percent of the profits from her business to charities and environmental organizations.

At eight years old, Maya started her own business making eco-friendly clothes and accessories. Now she is eighteen and the CEO of her own company, Maya's Ideas, which produces clothing made with organic, recycled, and vintage materials, as well as eco-safe non-toxic fruit and vegetable dyes. Sometimes Maya even uses herbals teas to dye her clothing!

Maya is also an artist and animator, and she loves drawing cartoons. She has been drawing since she was first able to hold a crayon, and her animated series, *The Pollinators*, is all about the importance of pollinators like bees to our environment.

Maya loves ideas! With ideas, she was able to turn scraps of material into hats, scarves, and bags. With ideas, she was able to turn her cartoons into films. And with ideas, she was able to create new things and start her own business. She has also been able to help educate other fashion brands on how to become more sustainable and ethical.

Maya's achievements include being named one of Oprah's Supersoul 100 changemakers, receiving a commendation from Barack Obama, being a TED speaker, and founding a nonprofit organization called Maya's Ideas 4 The Planet, where she designs and creates eco-friendly sanitary pads for women and girls living in countries in need. In 2016, Maya published her first book, *You Got This!*

Everything starts with an idea!

WASTE

HAVE YOU EVER wondered where all your trash goes?

Landfills, also known as garbage dumps, are places where the things we throw into our garbage bins—both at home and when we are out and about—get buried. They're usually just outside our biggest cities. Unfortunately, landfills pollute the environment, contaminate groundwater and soil, threaten wildlife, and produce greenhouse gases like methane and carbon dioxide.

The best way for you to help is by reducing the number of things you throw in the trash. There are all kinds of easy and fun ways to do this!

Everything we throw away has to go somewhere. Garbage all ends up in something called a landfill.

GREENHOUSE GASES

These are gases that trap heat and energy from the Sun, causing the temperature of Earth and the air above it to rise. Little by little, this rising temperature has devastating effects on animals and plants. It also causes sea levels to rise, creating more intense rains and hurricanes and hotter summers, and even expands the reach of infectious diseases.

DID YOU KNOW?

Every day, the average American creates nearly four and a half pounds of waste. Over one year, that's enough to fill a three-bedroom house!

MAKE A COMPOST BIN OR WORM FARM

More than half of the trash we put in our household bins is food scraps. Food scraps in landfills are one of the main causes of harmful greenhouse gases. By putting your food scraps in a compost bin or worm farm instead, you can significantly reduce the food waste you and your family send to the landfill. Composting also creates soil that is rich in nutrients, which you can use in your garden to make your plants grow big and strong.

Give it a go, and see if you can reduce the number of times you have to empty the bin!

HOW TO MAKE A COMPOST BIN

1. Decide where you're going to set up your compost—ideally, this should be somewhere dry and shady, where you can easily access water.

2. Find something to use as your compost bin. Old garbage bins and wooden boxes can work well. You can also set aside a patch of dirt surrounded by a ring of chicken wire if you have space outside.

3. Add a few brown and green layers (see "Carbon and Nitrogen") to get your compost started—try layering: brown, water, brown, green, brown, water, green, brown, and make your brown layers about three times as thick as your green layers.

4. Add water as often as needed to keep your compost moist but not too wet.

5. Use a spade to turn your pile once a week, moving the bottom layers up to the top. This helps mix air through your compost to keep it healthy.

6. That's it! Keep an old ice-cream container or small bucket in your kitchen so you can throw all your scraps into it. Empty this into your compost each day. When adding food scraps to your compost, it's a good idea to bury the new material under what's already there.

It can take anywhere from three to twelve months for the scraps you put in your compost to finish decomposing. You'll know when they're done because they will be dark and rich in color, and you won't be able to see any of the original materials. The compost mix will smell and look like sweet, earthy soil. It contains loads of nutrients—add it to any garden bed or potted plant to give your plants a boost.

— CARBON — AND NITROGEN

The best compost has a good balance of carbon **(brown)** and nitrogen **(green)**—about 3:1. Carbon and nitrogen are the magic ingredients in nature that help the microorganisms (like bacteria and fungi) digest your compost.

Brown layers include: dead leaves, mulch, straw, hay, twigs, shredded newspaper, and cardboard.

Green layers include: fresh grass clippings, clippings from plants with leaves, fruit and vegetable scraps, and coffee grinds.

TIP

Every time you add a green layer to your compost, add some brown over the top. This will help your compost decompose nicely.

WHAT CAN I
— PUT IN MY —
COMPOST?

YES: Fruits and veggies, garden scraps, eggshells, coffee and tea bags (remove the plastic tag), coffee grounds, shredded paper (not magazines, though), dead flowers, fallen leaves (in layers), wood and bamboo (like ice-cream sticks and toothbrushes), hair from your hairbrush, natural fibers like cotton and wool.

NO: Metal, plastic, glass, magazines, meat, dairy, fish, diseased plants.

NEWSPAPER BIN LINER

The good news is, when you're no longer putting your wet food scraps in the bin, you can line your bins with newspaper instead of plastic bin bags—or you may not need a bin liner at all.

Follow these instructions to make bags for smaller bins like those in an office, bedroom, or bathroom, using one or two large sheets of newspaper:

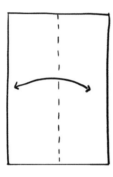

1. Fold to make a crease, then unfold.

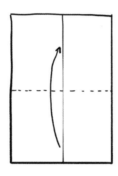

2. Fold along the dotted line.

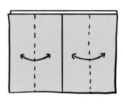

3. Fold to make creases, then unfold.

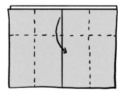

4. Fold along the dotted lines.

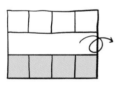

5. Turn over.

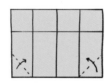

6. Fold along the dotted lines.

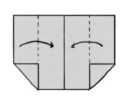

7. Fold along the dotted lines.

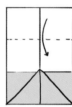

8. Fold along the dotted line.

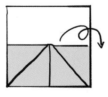

9. Turn over.

10. Open the pocket.

11. Finished!

THE COMPOST REVOLUTION

While there are composting councils and local organizations scattered all across the globe, the Compost Revolution—based in Australia—is a great example of a group that's making a difference.

The Compost Revolution is Australia's largest community of composters and worm farmers. They've helped over 41,700 households start diverting their waste from landfills, preventing over thirty-nine million pounds of greenhouse gas emissions. Working with 31 councils across Australia, The Compost Revolution offers discounted composting gear and delivers everything you need to your door. They then provide free online tutorials and support to help you get composting and become more self-sufficient, healthier, and happier!

What are your top tips for kids who want to start composting?

1. Composting and worm farming is one of the easiest and funnest ways to cut your family's trash in half. If you already recycle paper, glass, and plastic, then recycling food and garden waste at home is super easy. Just put it in your compost bin or worm farm and nature takes care of the rest! Plus, it's one of the only kinds of recycling you can do at home all by yourself.

2. A compost bin turns food and garden waste into rich soil for your garden and plants, while a worm farm turns food waste into both rich liquid fertilizer and soil. These are like super strong vitamins for growing delicious vegetables and fruit right at home.

3. You can also compost other natural materials like paper, hair, vacuum cleaner dust, fingernails, and old clothing. You can even compost pet waste! Just make sure you keep the right balance of greens (nitrogen) and browns (carbon), air, and moisture—then sit back as nature works its magic!

REUSE AND — REPURPOSE —

Get creative and inventive! Make new things from old things. Give value to the things you own.

Apart from food and kitchen scraps, there are lots of things that we throw away without even thinking: broken toys, clothes we've grown out of, empty bottles, glass jars, food containers, toilet rolls, egg cartons, milk bottles, tissue boxes—the list goes on.

Here are just a few examples of ways you can reuse these things. You can probably come up with lots of other ways.

GLASS JARS (such as empty honey, jam, peanut butter, or pasta sauce jars): use these to organize any small items you have; make pretty decorations by filling them with pebbles or shells; make a windproof candle; use them to store homemade jams, bath salts, or hair conditioner; store loose-leaf tea or other small food items like nuts and seeds in them; or sprout your own beans (see "Gardening and the Outdoors").

EGG CARTONS can be used to sprout seedlings, to sort your jewelry or other small items, or can be donated to local farmers or anyone you know with chickens. Note: if you sprout seedlings in an egg carton, you can then plant the whole carton in the soil (so long as it's made of cardboard). It will decompose!

OLD OR OUTGROWN CLOTHING can be cut into rags to use for cleaning. Use thicker items like jeans or corduroy garments to make patches to repair your other clothes. If an item is in good condition, donate it to your local thrift store or charity, or give it to a friend or family member. You can also donate old T-shirts to be turned into reusable bags—or try making your own bags out of them.

NEWSPAPER AND SCRAP PAPER can be used to line trash cans or used as the bottom layer of a garden bed (see "An Outdoor Garden"). Alternatively, you can shred it and add it to your compost or worm farm.

ICE-CREAM STICKS AND WOODEN SPOONS: write the names of your herbs and flowers on these and use them as plant markers.

REPURPOSING A SPRAY BOTTLE

There are lots of ways you can reuse an empty spray bottle, such as for personal care products, room fresheners, or household cleaning sprays. Choose a spray bottle that didn't contain any chemicals, and then wash it out. Also, keep your bottles for household and personal care separate. Try using your empty spray bottles for the following uses.

HYDRATING MIST

Fill your spray bottle with ⅓ purified water and ⅔ rosewater, then add a few drops of chamomile essential oil. Spray onto your face and skin for a refreshing, cooling mist.

Tip: You can also make your mist with cold chamomile, green or peppermint tea, witch hazel, cucumber juice, coconut water, aloe vera juice, vitamin E oil, and other essential oils such as lavender and ylang-ylang. Remember to use essential oils sparingly—you only need a few drops.

AIR FRESHENER

Simply mix water and a few drops of your favorite essential oils in your empty spray bottle, and then get spritzing!

HOUSEHOLD CLEANER

Fill a large spray bottle with ½ water, ½ white vinegar and ten drops of eucalyptus or tea tree oil. You can use this all around the house and in the bathroom to make everything fresh and clean.

ONE EARTH
NE CHANCE
FUTURE
VOTERS
WE A
RISI
CH
OUR
FUTUR
SKOLSTRE
FÖR
KLIMATE
CLIM
CH
IS
TOP

GRETA THUNBERG
Sweden

When eight-year-old Greta Thunberg first learned about climate change in 2011, she couldn't understand why so little was being done about it. If humanity's existence was at stake, why were people talking about anything else? By the age of eleven, Greta was in such deep despair that she became physically ill.

She shared her struggle with her parents and then educated them about climate change. They listened—her mother gave up flying, and her father became a vegetarian. That's when Greta realized she could make a difference.

"I think that if a few children can get headlines all over the world just by not going to school for a few weeks, imagine what we could all do together if we wanted to."

After seeing students strike in the United States, Greta came up with the idea of doing a similar strike for the climate. But no one was interested when she shared her idea to skip school every Friday and protest, rain or shine, in front of the Swedish parliament. So she made a sign and went by herself.

The second day Greta protested, several people joined her. There were even more the next day. News organizations caught wind of what she was doing, and within months Greta became an internationally recognized activist. Despite her shyness, she began speaking in front of crowds—and then important groups like the European Parliament, the World Economic Forum, and the United Nations. She met with world leaders like the Canadian prime minister and received the support of others, like the Pope and the German chancellor.

Greta inspired people around the world with her dedication, honesty, and vision. She played an important role during the Global Week of Climate Action: on September 20, 2019, four million people protested in 4,500 locations across 150 countries. In the past two years, she's received countless awards, becoming the youngest ever *TIME* magazine person of the year, and she's been nominated twice for the Nobel Peace Prize.

"The one thing we need more than hope is action. Once we start to act, hope is everywhere."

But Greta's message hasn't changed since she the first day of her school strike: Climate change is a crisis. Future generations are going to be most affected, even though they're the least responsible. World leaders aren't doing nearly enough. And everyone must act now to save the planet.

That message isn't always popular, however. World leaders have also criticized Greta, with some people even targeting her motives, physical appearance, or her diagnosis on the Autism spectrum. But it doesn't seem to bother her too much. "I have Asperger's," she's said in response to bullies. "And that means I'm sometimes a bit different from the norm. And—given the right circumstances—being different is a superpower."

Greta used to think she couldn't make a difference because she was too small. After all, what could one person do? But sometimes, one person is all it takes to inspire the world.

— BUYING LESS —
MEANS MORE
FOR THE PLANET

One of the biggest steps in reducing the number of things you throw away is to buy less. And one of the easiest ways to buy less is to avoid going to shopping centers unless you really need to. Try not to make shopping an activity that you do with your friends. Being surrounded by new and exciting things can make it hard to resist buying them. Instead, try to think of all the things you already own, and try to find other ways you can use them. If you do have to go to the shops, write a firm list of everything you need, and only buy what's on the list. Really think about what you're buying and whether you actually need it or just want it.

There are three simple things you can do whenever you're throwing anything away:

1. **STOP:** Before you throw anything in the trash, pause for a moment.

2. **THINK:** Is this something that you really need to throw away, or could you reuse it? Is it something that you could recycle, give to someone else, or put in a charity bin? Is it a food item or something that you could put in your compost bin or worm farm?

3. **ASK YOURSELF WHY:** Why do you have this item? Did you really need to buy it if you're now throwing it away? Is it made of plastic? Could you have avoided buying it?

Using these steps will make you more aware of your choices in the future and help you avoid buying things you don't really need.

CLEAN UP
BEACHES
AND
PARKS

HAVE YOU EVER done a clean-up day with your school? There are lots of clean-up events that your school can join—or why not start your own with your friends?

A cleaner world is a nicer world, and a safer place for plants and animals.

There is so much litter lying around—it looks terrible and can be harmful to native wildlife. When you see trash, put it in the bin. And if there isn't a bin nearby, take it home with you—never leave trash lying around.

By 2050 it's predicted that, by weight, there will be more plastic in the ocean than fish. An organization called Take 3 for the Sea aims to reduce global plastic pollution. They encourage everyone to take three pieces of trash with them whenever they leave a beach, waterway, or any other area, even if it's not your own trash. By doing this, you can make a difference.

RECYCLING

Most people are confused about what they can and can't recycle, so here's a quick guide. But remember: recycling is a last resort. The aim is not to have any items that need to be recycled in the first place!

You can put the following items in your curbside recycling bin:
- Hard plastic.
- Glass.
- Cardboard.
- Paper.
- Metal and cans (including aluminium cans, deodorant, and hairspray cans).
- Milk and juice cartons.

Things to remember:
- Make sure containers are empty.
- Both jars and their lids can be recycled, but keep them separate when putting them in your curbside bin.
- Keep items loose, not bundled together inside other items like bags or boxes.

HOW TO RECYCLE
— PLASTIC FILM —

Soft plastics cannot be recycled in the same way as hard plastics. Soft plastics include things like cookie sleeves, bread bags, bubble wrap, pet-food bags, cereal-box liners, chocolate and snack wrappers, chip bags, cling wrap, rice and pasta bags, zip lock bags, and single-use plastic bags.

The good news is that there are thousands of places where you can drop off soft plastics to be recycled. These are typically located at supermarkets, hardware stores, or recycling centers, and you may have one in your area. You can find your nearest drop-off point on the website plasticfilmrecycling.org.

Do the scrunch test: if it's soft plastic and can be scrunched into a ball, it can be recycled—just not in your typical recycling bin!

If you don't have access to a soft plastics recycling bin at a participating supermarket, don't worry. Just knowing that soft plastics can't be included with your home recycling means you'll be able to make better decisions to avoid them in the future.

While it's good to dispose of plastic responsibly, it's better to avoid plastic altogether. Soft plastics can also only be recycled once, which means that they will still end up in the landfill eventually.

Recycling is also not as simple as it's made out to be, and the recycling industry has some major problems, which lead to much of our recyclable waste ending up in landfills. So the best way to solve the issue of waste is to reduce the amount you produce in the first place.

TIP

A lot of toys are made from plastic, and while they're lots of fun, you probably won't use them forever. Have a go at sorting your toys into those that are made from plastic and those that aren't.

Work out which toys are your favorites and look after them so you don't need to throw them away and get new ones. When your toys break, see if you can fix them instead of throwing them away, and if you really don't need them anymore, donate them to charity.

ELIF BILGIN
Turkey

Elif Bilgin has always loved learning. She taught herself how to read when she was four years old so she could start reading science books. Then, when she was eight, she began inventing; her first project was making window wipers for her glasses.

At fourteen years old, she wanted to do something to help reduce plastic pollution in the Bosphorus, the main waterway in her hometown of Istanbul in Turkey. When she started researching, she found that Thailand throws away thousands of pounds of banana peels every day. This gave her an idea. She decided to invent a way to turn banana peels into bioplastic.

Elif started experimenting. It took her two years and twelve experiments, ten of which failed, before she was finally successful. She then entered her project into the Google Science in Action award, and she won!

Along with winning $50,000 in prize money, Elif inspired many more young people to be creative and look for out-of-the-box ideas to save the planet.

TAKE 3 FOR THE SEA

Take 3 for the Sea believes in simple actions to solve difficult problems. With the combined knowledge of marine ecologist Roberta Dixon-Valk, youth educator Amanda Marechal, and environmentalist Tim Silverwood, Take 3 was launched in 2010 with the mission to reduce global plastic pollution by educating and inspiring people to participate and help solve the problem.

What are your top tips for kids who want to reduce plastic pollution?

1. **Education:** Through education, Take 3 is building a movement of people connected to the planet. When people understand the problem, they become inspired to act!

2. **Participation:** Take 3 pieces of trash with you when you leave the beach, waterway, or . . . anywhere and you have made a difference.

3. **Join the movement:** Share your #Take3fortheSea photos with your friends and family and encourage them to share theirs too. Every piece of trash removed from the environment creates a healthier, happier planet. Protecting our planet is everyone's concern, and simple actions when multiplied can have a big impact.

FOOD

FOOD MAKES EVERYONE happy. It's delicious, makes us feel good, and brings us all together at mealtimes. But it's also one of the main contributors when it comes to using plastic and generating waste. You probably sometimes read the labels on your food or check the ingredients, and you might often see a lot of words you've never even heard of before or can't pronounce. Well, you're not alone—even adults have no idea what many of those things are.

Some of the things we can all do to help change the world include learning where our food comes from, what it's made from, shopping from local sources, buying only what we need, and using all our food so we don't contribute to food waste.

Along with learning to cut down our plastic use and waste, we need to make sure we're eating food that comes from a good place and was produced in an environmentally friendly and ethical way.

SUPERMARKETS VS. FARMERS' MARKETS

THE MOST IMPORTANT thing about food is knowing where it comes from. Is it local, or did it have to travel hundreds of miles to get to you? When you're buying meat, fruits, and vegetables from a supermarket, it can be hard to find out exactly where it came from or what processes went into growing it.

But when you buy from farmers' markets, you can get a much better idea of all the steps that went into getting the food to you, and you can often meet the farmers who grew the food. Farmers are an incredible source of information about the food you eat.

Here are six questions you might want to ask a farmer next time you see them at a market:

- What do you use to keep away pests and weeds?
- What kind of fertilizers do you use?
- How long ago was your produce harvested?
- What do your animals eat?
- How much fresh air and exercise do your animals get?
- Can I come and visit your farm?

Knowing where your food comes from can also help you understand how it was grown and what it's made from.

Most farmers' markets, and some stores, sell what's sometimes called "ugly" or "imperfect" fruit and vegetables. Incredibly, 40 percent of the fruits and vegetables produced in America are rejected by supermarkets because they don't look perfect, even though they still taste the same. So when you see a lemon that's a bit too round, a carrot that's a bit bent, an orange with a brown patch or a strawberry that looks out of shape, don't assume there's something wrong with it. It's just as good as any other fruit, and by buying it, you're stopping these delicious fruits and vegetables from going to waste.

THE DIFFERENT TYPES OF EGGS

YOU'VE PROBABLY HEARD eggs being described in a few different ways: cage, free-range, pasture-raised. Maybe you've even heard about the size of the spaces that chickens are sometimes kept in, with thousands of hens often being squeezed into cramped, uncomfortable spaces. It's hard to tell from the packaging which eggs are the best ones to buy, but here are a few helpful tips.

- Be wary of the terms "farm fresh," "all natural," and "cage-free." Chickens raised in these conditions don't get to go outside and spread their wings—they often have to remain in one small space for their entire lives.
- Look for pastured or pasture-raised eggs—this usually means the chickens have space to roam and forage outside in fields and eat the bugs and grass they like.
- Organic eggs: while these chickens are not fed synthetic pesticides, hormones, or antibiotics, the space they live in is often very small. Always research the farm to find out how big the space is and how many chickens are living in it.

HOW MANY CHICKENS
— PER ACRE? —

Terms like "free range" aren't very meaningful in the United States. For that label, the only legal requirement is that chickens have some kind of access to the outdoors—which in some cases can just be a hole for the chickens to stick their heads outside!

Instead, a better way to know how chickens are treated is by how many chickens are being raised on each acre. The fewer birds per acre, the better. For example, if a farm wants to be Certified Humane® "Pasture Raised" by the independent organization Humane Farm Animal Care, they can't have more than four hundred birds per acre. That comes out to 108 square feet of outdoor pasture per bird, while the vast majority of hens in America are raised in a cage with less than *half a square foot* of space for their entire lives.

— WHAT YOU CAN DO —

- Buy eggs locally, so you can find out exactly what conditions the chickens are living in, what they eat, how much time they spend outside, and how much space they have.
- Go to farmers' markets and ask the farmers questions about how they treat their chickens.
- If you have space, you could even look into getting your own chickens.

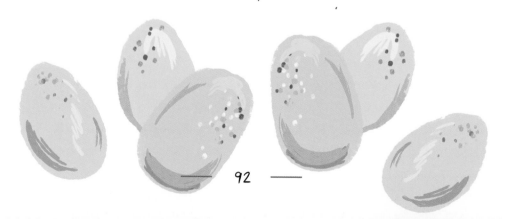

KATIE STAGLIANO
United States of America

Katie Stagliano has a dream to end hunger and she has a healthy solution. Her dream began when she was in the third grade and she and her brother each received a cabbage seedling. They planted their seedlings in the backyard. As Katie cared for her little cabbage seedling, it began to grow. It grew bigger and bigger until she had to get her grandfather to help her build a cage around it so wild animals wouldn't eat it. Eventually, the cabbage grew to weigh over forty pounds.

But what would Katie do with her special cabbage? The answer came to her one night at the dinner table: she would give it to families in need.

She donated the cabbage to a local soup kitchen, where it was used it to feed 275 guests!

From there, she started Katie's Krops, which empowers kids to make their own vegetable gardens. Now thousands of children are looking after more than one hundred Katie's Krops gardens and helping to end hunger in their communities. In 2018, Katie's Krops donated more than 38,000 pounds of fresh produce to those in need.

Katie even wrote her own award-winning children's book, *Katie's Cabbage.*

THE MEAT INDUSTRY

WHEN BUYING MEAT from a supermarket, you don't know how the animal was raised; how it was treated; what kinds of food, antibiotics, or hormones it was fed; or whether it even got to go outside. Sadly, the meat industry can be a cruel place, where animals are not treated well.

There are two things you can do to help with this. Firstly, you can try to reduce the amount of meat you eat. Reducing the amount of meat you eat also makes a huge difference to the environment. Livestock such as cows and sheep produce methane gas, which is a greenhouse gas. Eating less meat means fewer animals are raised, which in turn reduces the greenhouse gases being produced.

Secondly, you can buy your meat from a local butcher or farmers' market instead of a supermarket. Buying from a butcher or farmers' market means you can find out how the animal was treated and make sure you're not supporting cruelty to animals.

TIP

When reducing the amount of meat you eat, make sure you get your protein from other sources instead. Remember to eat more foods like lentils, beans, chickpeas, and nuts to ensure you get the nutrition you need.

JOSH MURRAY
Australia

The average age of a farmer in Australia is fifty-six. Josh Murray started selling eggs from his family's farm when he was only nine! He started with local shops, then moved on to farmers' markets. Now that he is eighteen, Josh runs Josh's Rainbow Eggs, a farm that produces 55,000 pasture-raised eggs per week. He stresses how important it is that his chickens are treated ethically, and says that each flock of chickens has its own personality traits.

1. How old are you now, and how old were you when you started your egg business?

I'm eighteen, and I was nine when I started my egg business.

2. Where did you grow up, and how did that inspire you?

When I was six, Mom and Dad bought our 120-acre farm in the Macedon Ranges, and the first animals we got were hens and guinea pigs. Otherwise, I'd never have started my egg business. Also Mom homeschooled me, and she saw my egg business as an amazing opportunity to learn important skills. She didn't realize it would turn into such a big business!

3. What inspired you to start your business?

When I was nine years old, Mom said, "Why don't you do all the work with the hens and then you can have all the money from the eggs?" We had forty hens, which didn't seem much work, so I gladly agreed. Initially, I sold eggs to our neighbors for $3/dozen. Then I expanded my flock and realized I needed new customers. The name came when a friend opened a carton that, as well as brown and white eggs, included some blue and green Araucana eggs and even a pinkish egg. She said, "You have rainbow eggs!" And so it became Josh's Rainbow Eggs. I started cold-calling shops in the nearby town of Gisborne, selling my eggs to the employees. That went well so I got more hens and went to farmers' markets, and a year or so later to local independent supermarkets. The big leap was approaching Coles Supermarkets in 2014. The National Category Manager was great, and within a few months we were delivering eggs direct to Coles in our local area. The business took off. Now, four years later, the farm has ten thousand hens and we deliver to twenty-four Coles and fifteen Woolworths stores and twelve independent supermarkets.

4. Tell us about Josh's Rainbow Eggs.

We produce truly free-range eggs. Over nine years, we believe we've developed the most environmentally sustainable model of egg farming in Australia. Our innovative farming system is both ecologically regenerative and ethical. Hens sleep in small, mobile, solar-powered sheds, rotated across the paddock. Eggs are delivered direct from our farm to Coles and Woolworths stores in regional Victoria and Melbourne. We visit each store weekly, engage directly with customers, and on special occasions even bring our hens to the stores for kids to cuddle. We created an egg donation platform with Foodbank where our customers can gift eggs directly to families in need, and we donate eggs directly. I've given talks to thousands of schoolchildren about my egg business and I'm about to launch an on-farm education and research program that will allow children to see firsthand a truly environmentally sustainable farm. With the help of researchers and educators, I'm designing curriculum materials on sustainable agriculture. I'm also writing a book for children about my story, and I hope to inspire a whole generation of young people.

5. Why is it important to buy free-range, ethical eggs?

Being a hen means scratching, pecking, and dust bathing. Hens can't do this inside a shed or inside a cage. So for a hen to express her innate behaviors, she must be outside on pasture. Hen welfare is number one to me. I provide what I believe to be the best life a hen can have. Our hens live in small flocks, which makes it much less stressful on them as they know each other. Our hens always have access to fresh pasture and all go outside each day. Also, after they're no longer laying for us, we give them away to backyarders, so they can live for many more years.

6. What is your biggest achievement so far?

Our partnership with Foodbank. In two years, we've donated over 250,000 eggs to families in Victoria, Australia. Also, I won the People's Choice Award in 2018 at the Victorian Young Achiever Awards. This demonstrated how much my customers love my eggs, how loyal they are, and that they will take time to vote for me. I was most honored.

7. **Do you have any tips for the best way to buy eggs?**

If you can't buy my eggs, then research the brand. Transparency is important—the business should have a website and Facebook page with photos and a description of their philosophy. It's important to know how they look after their hens and what type of farm they run. Then, as a consumer, you can make an informed choice.

8. **What's your favorite thing about chickens?**

I love the sounds they make. Their sounds are happy and curious, and they're always busy searching for bugs and tasty things to eat. Some hens have unique personalities. We once had a hen we called Tractor Chook, as every time we were in the pasture in the tractor, she'd jump up and climb in the window and sit on the little kid's seat.

SUSTAINABLE

FISH

THE WORLD'S OCEANS are vast and beautiful places. They're home to some incredibly diverse ecosystems, including lush shorelines, stunning coral reefs, wide open oceans, and the mysterious deep ocean, where there's no light at all. But our oceans are being threatened by overfishing.

Overfishing is when fish are removed from the water so fast, and in such huge numbers, that the species can't replenish itself. This has major effects on the ecosystem the fish live in, as many other sea creatures also rely on those fish for food.

Because many of the fish we catch are herbivores, coral reefs are also in danger, because overfishing means there aren't enough fish left to eat the algae and maintain the delicate balance of the reefs. In short, overfishing has devastating effects on marine ecosystems.

> We need to help raise awareness of the dangers of overfishing and encourage people to use, and support, more sustainable fishing methods.

Sustainable seafood refers to methods of fishing that have a minimal impact on fish populations and the marine environment. Fish can be wild caught from fast-growing species, using approaches that won't damage ecosystems or other sea creatures. They can also be farmed in aquaculture, which means they're grown in small systems that don't destroy ocean habitats.

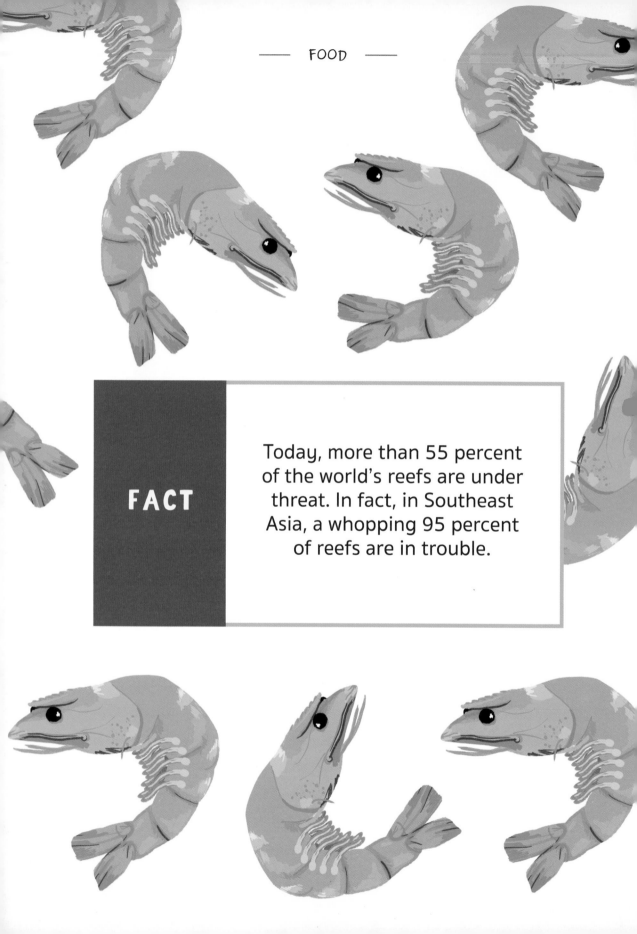

FACT

Today, more than 55 percent of the world's reefs are under threat. In fact, in Southeast Asia, a whopping 95 percent of reefs are in trouble.

— WHAT YOU — CAN DO

- Start a conversation: always talk to the fishmonger, supermarket assistant, or waiter before you choose seafood. Some questions you could ask are:
  - Do you know if the species is fished in sustainable numbers?
  - Do you know whether the methods used to catch the fish were designed to minimize damage to the environment and other marine wildlife?
- Join a campaign to make sure seafood is labeled correctly, telling people what species of fish it is, where it's from, and how it was caught or farmed.
- Write a letter to a newspaper, start your own petition, contact your local representative, or just raise awareness in your own community. Make your voice heard!

You might also want to visit the website for the Monterey Bay Aquarium Seafood Watch guide or download the app to start learning more about what you can do.

PACKING AN ECO-FRIENDLY LUNCH

MAKING YOUR LUNCH eco-friendly involves avoiding both plastic packaging and creating waste. Start by buying a stainless-steel lunch box, then go from there. A bento box with different compartments can be a great idea—that way you don't have to use more wrapping to separate your food.

Here are some ideas to get you started:

- Eat food that comes in its own natural packaging, like bananas and apples. Fruit doesn't need to come in plastic—it's already wrapped! And remember to take your fruit scraps home to compost them.
- Avoid foods that are individually wrapped in soft plastics, such as snack and chocolate bars.
- To reduce packaging, make your own granola bars, cookies, or savory muffins, and buy nuts in bulk.
- When you buy bread for your sandwiches, get it from a bakery and bring your own bag. You could even have a go at making your own bread!

TIPS

- Always use your leftovers—don't throw them away. Store them in the fridge and eat them later, or put them on your compost.
- Organize your fridge so the things that will spoil first are at the front.
- Buy "ugly" fruits and veggies, and try to buy foods that are in season. Look at the Seasonal Food Guide website to see what's in season in your state.
- When you go to restaurants, take a reusable container with you and ask if you can take any leftover food home for lunch the next day.

USE WHAT YOU'VE GOT

When it comes to food, one of the most important things is to use what you've got. Before you buy more food, see if you can get creative and make something out of the things you have on hand, especially fruits and vegetables. Before your parents throw away (or compost) any old fruits and veggies, see if you can use them for these recipes.

RECIPE

STOCK

Making stock is a great way to use all your old vegetables or leftover meat bones. The stock can then be used to make things like soups, stews, sauces, pies, and risottos.

You'll need:
- Vegetables, such as onions, celery, carrots, turnips, parsnips, leeks, shallots, and herbs.
- Bay leaves.
- Leftover chicken, beef, or lamb bones (optional).

What to do:
1. Roughly chop all your ingredients and place them in a large saucepan. You don't even need to peel them!
2. Add enough water to just cover all your ingredients.
3. Put the saucepan on the stove on medium–high heat and bring to a boil.
4. Turn the heat down to low and allow to simmer for at least one to two hours. The longer the better!
5. Remove from heat and strain the liquid into another saucepan or container.
6. Your stock can be stored in the fridge for three to four days or frozen for six months.

To turn your stock into a delicious chicken noodle soup, add chicken, corn, pasta, chopped carrots, fresh herbs, and a bit of salt, and cook them in your stock. Also add any fresh vegetables you like.

Tip: Use a potato masher to crush all your vegetables in the liquid before straining your stock. This will ensure you get the maximum flavor from your ingredients. Just be careful: the liquid will be hot!

APPLE CRUMBLE

If your apples get too old to eat, you don't need to throw them away. A great way to use old apples, or a combination of fruits like pears, peaches, berries, or plums, is to make a crumble.
Serves 5–6.

You'll need:

Filling:
- 4 medium apples.
- ½ cup white sugar.
- 1 teaspoon ground cinnamon.
- 2 tablespoons lemon juice.

Topping:
- 1 cup rolled oats.
- 1 cup all-purpose flour.
- ¾ cup brown sugar.
- 1 teaspoon ground cinnamon.
- 7 tablespoons unsalted butter, melted.

What to do:

1. Preheat oven to 350°F.

2. Peel and core the apples (remember to put the peelings in your compost or worm farm), then roughly chop them into half-inch cubes.

3. Place the apple cubes in a baking dish and toss with sugar, cinnamon, and lemon juice.

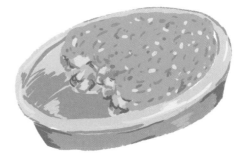

4. To prepare the topping, mix all topping ingredients together in a bowl with your fingers until clumps form, then spread over the top of your apple mixture.

5. Bake for 30 to 40 minutes, or until the crumble is golden brown. Allow to stand for 10 minutes before serving.

6. Serve warm with vanilla ice cream.

HOMEMADE STRAWBERRY JAM

Jam is really easy to make and an excellent way to use your leftover berries if they're starting to get too old to eat. And better yet, you can store your jam in a repurposed jar, and even give it as a gift!

You'll need:

- 1 pound strawberries, leaves removed.
- 1½ cups powdered sugar.
- ½ tablespoon lemon zest.
- 1 tablespoon lemon juice.
- 1 repurposed jam jar (sterilize by boiling in water for 10 minutes).

What to do:

1. Place strawberries, powdered sugar, lemon zest, and juice in a saucepan and gently crush with a potato masher.

2. Place the saucepan on low heat and simmer until sugar dissolves. The sugar must be completely dissolved, or your jam will not set correctly and may have lumps of sugar.

3. Turn the heat up to medium–high and allow the mixture to boil rapidly for 10 minutes, stirring often. Use a long wooden spoon when stirring, and watch out as boiling jam may spit.

4. Do the wrinkle test: spoon a little jam onto a cold plate, wait for 30 seconds, then push it with your finger. If the jam wrinkles up, it's ready, but if it spreads back out, keep boiling it for another 2 minutes or until the jam wrinkles when cooled.

5. Pour your jam into the jam jar and allow to cool completely before sealing. Be very careful—the jam will be extremely hot! You may want to ask an adult for help with this part. Store in fridge until eaten.

GARDENING AND THE OUTDOORS

DID **YOU** **KNOW** that being outdoors actually makes you happier? Studies have shown that spending just fifteen minutes in nature—doing things like listening to the birds, identifying plant species, looking at the sky, or smelling the sunshine—will make you happier and more relaxed, creative, and focused. So get into some green spaces and give your mood a boost!

One of the best ways to experience nature and help change the world is to start your own garden. Whether you live on a big property, a small block, or in an apartment, there are ways for you to start gardening.

AN

OUTDOR

#

THE FIRST STEP is to work out where you're going to start your garden. This will help determine what kind of plants you can grow.

Almost all flowering plants, including fruit and vegetables, need at least five or six hours of sunlight each day to grow, so if your garden gets absolutely no sun, it's probably best to stick with plants that prefer moist soil. These will often have deep green leaves. On the other hand, if your garden is in full sun, on very hot summer days, even plants that like sun will need some afternoon shade.

Always research your plants before you put them in the ground—find out how much water they need, what kind of soil they like (and whether it's moist or well drained), and how tall they will grow.

If you want to grow edible plants, aim for a spot that gets morning sun and afternoon shade.

WHAT PLANTS SHOULD I CHOOSE?

FULL SUN	PART SUN	FULL SHADE
Basil	Chives	Ferns
Rosemary	Mint	Elephant ear
Parsley	Cilantro	Foxgloves
Sage	Lettuce	Hellebores
Thyme	Kale	Bluebells
Tomatoes	Spinach	Forget-Me-Nots
Corn	Carrots	Anthuriums
Beans	Potatoes	Azaleas
Squash	Parsnips	Mona Lavender
Cucumbers	Beets	Fire Lily/Peace Lily
Peppers	Strawberries	Sweet Box
Lavender	Pansies	Native Violets
Marigolds	Hydrangeas	Lady Gowrie Camellia
Geraniums	Begonias	New Zealand Rock Lily
Nasturtiums	Gardenias	Winter Daphne

START YOUR OWN OUTDOOR GARDEN

Decide where you want to set up your garden. You might already have some garden beds, but if not, you could ask your parents to buy raised garden beds or planter boxes.

Raised garden beds have lots of advantages: they stop weeds from getting into your garden; water drains well, so plant roots don't rot; and the soil also warms up quicker than the soil in garden beds, which helps plants grow.

If you prefer to dig your garden bed straight into the soil, mark out the area and turn the soil carefully with a spade to loosen it. Then line the perimeter of your turned earth, cover it with newspaper and hay, add compost, and get planting! Make sure you water your garden regularly.

Ask a parent or guardian to help you follow these instructions, and remember: start small! Learn to grow a few simple things first, then you can move on to different plants.

STARTING AN OUTDOOR GARDEN

1. Remember to choose a spot that gets at least five hours of sunlight every day. If this isn't possible, see the chart on page 115 for other kinds of plants you can grow. Also keep in mind that you'll need regular access to water, so try to choose a spot that's near a hose or tap.

2. Mark out the area for your garden bed. Try to make sure it's no wider than four feet, so you can always reach the middle of your garden without stepping on the plants.

3. Prepare the soil using a spade and a pitchfork to turn the grass over and loosen up the dirt. This will give you better drainage.

4. Cover the turned earth with a few sheets of wet cardboard, newspaper or hay, or cloth. Keeping these materials wet will ensure they don't suck moisture out of the soil.

5. Line the perimeter of your garden. You can use rot-resistant wooden boards, logs, or bricks, or get creative and use rocks to mark the area. If you don't want to line it, you can simply build your mound of soil directly onto your chosen area.

6. Fill your bed with a combination of soil from your local hardware store or nursery, compost, and native soil.

7. After you've put your plants in, you can also cover your garden bed with mulch to keep those pesky weeds away, help maintain moisture, and protect your soil.

— PUTTING — YOUR PLANTS IN THE GROUND

After you've set up your garden bed and chosen your plants, it's time to put them in the ground. If you've followed the steps above, your soil should be ready to go. If you're planting in another garden bed, make sure the soil is loosened up so the roots can get through. Pull out any grass or weeds and, if possible, enrich your soil with compost.

1. Dig a hole slightly larger than the pot your plant is in. You can put the pot in the hole to make sure it's the right size.

2. Gently squeeze the sides of the pot to release the plant. Then, holding the base of your plant, turn the pot upside down and give the pot another squeeze until your plant comes out. Do not pull the plant out by its stem or leaves. You want to keep as much of the potting mix around the roots as you can. Try not to touch or disturb the roots.

3. Place your plant in the hole, and carefully refill the rest of the hole. Firmly press the soil down around the plant to keep it steady.

4. Always give plants a good soaking with water as soon as you've finished planting them.

5. To help your plant get used to its new home, water at least once a day for the first one to two weeks. Add a little bit of worm juice from your worm farm.

FELIX FINKBEINER
Germany

When Felix Finkbeiner was just nine years old, he created Plant-for-the-Planet, an organization that raises awareness among children about climate change.

Felix's journey started when he had to prepare a classroom presentation on climate change. To Felix, climate change meant danger to his favorite type of animal: polar bears. When he started researching for his assignment, he found out about a woman named Wangari Maathai from Kenya, the first African woman to be awarded the Nobel Peace Prize. Wangari planted thirty million saplings in thirty years to help recover some of Africa's bare land with trees.

Felix was inspired to start his own mission—to get children all over the world to plant trees. His goal was one million trees per country. Trees take in carbon dioxide and produce oxygen, so this would help offset all harmful carbon dioxide emissions. Three years later, in Germany, the children planted the one millionth tree. They were on track to realizing Felix's goal.

But Felix didn't stop there. When he was ten years old, he spoke in the European Parliament, and when he was thirteen, he spoke at the UN General Assembly. Felix is now twenty-one years old, and his project has seen more than fifteen billion trees get planted around the world. Now, Plant-for-the-Planet has a new goal: one trillion trees.

More than seventy thousand of the children who help Felix are ambassadors for climate justice, and they are between nine and twelve years old. Plant-for-the-Planet plants a new tree every fifteen seconds. Incredible! So it's time to stop talking and get planting.

A

BALCONY

GARDEN

BALCONY GARDENS ARE a wonderful way to bring some green space to your apartment, as well as make it possible for you to grow your own food.

It's important to choose plants that are right for the kind of sunlight you get on your balcony. You might want to spend a few days monitoring how much sun your balcony gets throughout the day. Remember to write down your observations.

How to choose a pot: Choose the biggest pot that you have space for. The more soil the pot holds, the more moisture it will hold, and this will stop your plants drying out. Always buy pots that have drainage holes, then place the pots in a tray or line the bottom with cloth so the soil doesn't spill out. You can also get hanging pots that go on hooks or pots that can hook onto the railing of your balcony.

Buy potting mix from your local nursery, and don't forget to add in your extra-good compost mix if you have some—your plants will love it.

Once you've assessed how much sunlight you get, and when, it's time to pick your plants and your pots.

Herbs grow well in pots, and so do many types of flowers, fruits, and veggies. Here are some of the easiest plants to grow in pots (but remember to check how much sunlight you get!):

- **Herbs:** rosemary, mint, parsley, and chives.
- **Fruits/Veggies:** lettuce and salad leaves, cucumbers, tomatoes, strawberries, dwarf citrus trees.
- **Flowers:** marigolds, lavender, geraniums, begonias.
- **Succulents:** all succulent species, but especially aloe vera.

There are many benefits of balcony pots: apart from regular watering, they don't need much maintenance; you can move your pots around to make sure they're in the best place with the right amount of sunlight; and if you move, you can take your plants with you!

Above all, watering is KEY. One of the main reasons balcony plants die is lack of water. Unless your balcony plants get plenty of rain, you will need to water them pretty much every day. Just remember, different plants like different amounts of moisture, so check how much water your plants need.

Don't forget to feed your plants, too—adding some slow-release plant food once or twice a year will keep your plants healthy. If you have a worm farm, remember to use that nutritious, organic worm juice on your plants.

TIP

Take note of how tall your plants will grow: if they grow too tall, they will shade the plants nearby. So, arrange your pots carefully to ensure they get enough sunlight.

GROWING PLANTS INDOORS

EVEN IF YOU HAVE limited outdoor space at home, you can still start your own garden. An excellent way to start is by growing your own microgreens. Microgreens are seeds growing in soil that have burst open, become green, and developed their first leaves. They are the next stage of a plant after a sprout. Microgreens are extremely healthy—you can use them to garnish your dinner, eat them in salads, put them on pizza or avocado toast, or just add them to a sandwich. You can eat them with pretty much anything!

GROWING YOUR OWN MICROGREENS

A great way to reuse clear plastic containers from buying berries or cherry tomatoes is to grow microgreens and sprout herbs. You just need access to good light, like a windowsill or a table near a glass door.

MICROGREENS

You'll need:

- Organic seeds such as basil, beetroot, broccoli, cabbage, celery, coriander, kale, lettuce, mustard, parsley, peas, radish, rocket, spinach, and many others.
- A repurposed plastic clamshell.
- Soil from your compost, local nursery, or hardware store.
- A repurposed spray bottle.
- Scissors.

What to do:

1. Prepare your seeds by soaking them in warm water for a couple of hours.

2. Meanwhile, fill your plastic clamshell about three-fourths full with soil. Add a little water to the soil to make it moist. Put the clamshell on a plate to stop soil and water leaking.

3. When your seeds have finished soaking, sprinkle them over the soil, and then cover them with a small amount of dry soil. The dry soil covering only needs to be about a quarter inch deep.

4. Once seeds start sprouting, lightly mist your plants regularly to keep the soil moist but not too wet. You can close the lid of your clamshell to keep the air nice and humid for your seeds to grow.

5. When your seedlings are anywhere from one to four inches tall, use scissors to cut the stems just above the soil. They're ready to eat!

DID YOU KNOW?

The coriander seeds that your parents might have in their spice rack can actually be planted and will grow into cilantro plants.

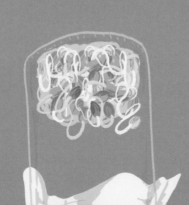

SPROUTING YOUR OWN BEANS AND LEGUMES

Along with repurposing your plastic clamshells, you can reuse glass jars to sprout your own beans and legumes. Sprouts are the very first growth that you see after a seed is planted.

You'll need:

- 1–2 tablespoons dried beans or legumes. You can get these at any bulk food store. The best ones are mung beans, lentils, and chickpeas.
- A repurposed glass jar.
- A kitchen cloth and a rubber band.

What to do:

1. Rinse the beans and place them in the jar.

2. Fill the jar with water.

3. Put the kitchen cloth over the top of the jar and seal it tightly with a rubber band. Leave overnight.

4. The next morning, turn the jar upside down and let the water slowly drain out. Leave until night. At night, fill up the jar with water again, then reseal the jar with the cloth and rubber band.

5. Repeat this process morning and night until the beans sprout.

6. Once the tails have reached twice the length of the bean you've chosen, replace the cloth with the jar lid and refrigerate until eaten. Do not store for longer than five days.

— TOP —
INDOOR
PLANT
IDEAS

- Swiss cheese plant.
- Lucky bamboo.
- Peace lily.
- Bromeliad.
- Zanzibar gem.

— COMMUNITY — GARDENS

If you live in an apartment that has limited outdoor space, there may be a community garden nearby that you can participate in. Community gardens are places where local people can come together to help look after garden beds producing fruit, vegetables, flowers, plants, and trees. They bring neighborhoods together, provide fresh food, enhance people's sense of wellbeing, support bees and other native creatures, and help reduce the effects of climate change.

Community gardens can also give you access to compost or a worm farm!

RUBY THE CLIMATE KID

Australia

Ruby is a nine-year-old girl from the Gamilaraay nation, an Indigenous Australian people group. She loves the planet and is determined to do all she can to save it—and get as many other people to help her as she can!

1. How old are you now and how old were you when you started being the Climate Kid?

I am nine years old. I became "The Climate Kid" when I was five years old after I learned about the rate of extinction of our amazing wildlife around the world. The Western Black Rhino and its extinction was in a documentary I was watching, and then I found out it's because of us—humans—that so many species have become extinct. I couldn't believe that we could be the reason that animals were dying, so I had to find out why.

My parents showed me documentaries and information on the internet, and I read so many books on wildlife, marine life, and climate change. I learned as much as I could, because I wanted to be smart and find ways to save the planet.

I decided to start filming my own videos for kids like me so we could learn together. Then my mom asked me what I wanted people to call me, and I said Ruby the Climate Kid so everyone would know that I was going to tell them about climate change and how we can save the planet.

It is very upsetting to learn that humans have let this happen by making bad decisions.

The reason I became the Climate Kid is to raise awareness and show that a kid can make a difference. I am a kid, but the grown-ups around me listen to me and help me with my ideas so we can make better decisions. The kids at my school and in my community are becoming more aware, and we even have an environmental club at my school.

2. Where did you grow up, and how did that inspire you?

I live in Engadine, on Dharawal country, which is right beside the national park. The national park inspires me because I can see the beauty of the natural world and feel strongly about protecting it, knowing that it is a provider of oxygen and life for the wildlife living in it.

3. What is your favorite hobby or pastime?

I have so many hobbies, but I do really love hiking and gardening. I'm learning all about plants as I grow more and more from seeds at home. I'm planting them in my garden and giving them to people to grow in theirs—every seed is an opportunity to bring new plants to life. When I go hiking, it's so interesting to see new plants and trees growing and see that there is not a pattern or deliberate way that they're growing—but that they're growing from the spot their seed fell from a higher plant.

4. Tell us about what you do to save the planet.

I try to learn more and more and have conversations with grown-ups every day about choices we make that can be made better. I talk to my parents about things we can do at home to reduce, reuse, and recycle, and they listen and work with me to start doing things better.

I talk to teachers and other grown-ups I know. I told my great-grandpa Tom about how I have been saving seeds from my fruit and germinating them and growing them into trees, and he was very happy with my efforts. I gave him a lemon tree and orange tree, and they are growing in his backyard now.

I also use social media to share ideas, write my thoughts, and show people what is happening around the world. I think as more people become aware of the devastation, they will be more active in trying to change.

I write to politicians and companies, urging them to make better choices for our planet. I have written to the prime minister and urged him to invest in renewables and stop the destructive mining practices that are harming our ecosystems. When I write to companies, I ask them to be mindful of how harmful plastic is and ask them to find better ways to package their products that are sustainable.

5. What is your biggest achievement so far?

I have grown apple trees from seeds, and now they are taller than my mom. I have made sustainable fabric bags, and now there are a heap of people using my bags that don't need to use plastic bags. I have raised money for organizations that are trying to save the planet.

But I don't really have a big achievement. I just want to keep raising awareness and pressure grown-ups to make better choices. I also want grown-ups to pressure the government to take more action on climate change.

6. What is your favorite animal and why?

This is a hard question. I absolutely love black rhinos because I think they're gentle like puppies and so innocent. It makes me upset that they are hunted and so many other species are now extinct or vulnerable.

Otters are really cheeky, and they make my mom smile, so I love them. I think that our Australian mammals are some of the most incredible and interesting animals—they are marvels of evolution. For example, the wombat's pouch is backward so that when they dig, the dirt doesn't go in the pouch and suffocate the baby. Just so incredible.

7. Do you have any tips for other kids who want to help save the planet?

Learn as much as you can and join other kids to do it together. Speak to grown-ups and show them how little decisions every day can make a difference, such as using less plastic, using less electricity and water, wasting less, and making smarter decisions with transportation.

Be green and grow plants—we can save the planet one plant at a time.

Billions of trees are cut down every month, so we need to grow and grow and grow and know that our actions together amount to something very big. Our plants are essential to us having air to breathe so we have to protect them and stop allowing them to be cut down when there are alternatives such as bamboo, recycling, and renewables.

GROWING ORGANIC FOOD

By growing your own food, you also reduce the emissions produced by trucks carrying food to shops and supermarkets.

ORGANIC FOOD IS food that's grown without the use of chemical fertilizers or pesticides. These toxic chemicals can be harmful—they are designed to kill everything but the plant. Growing organic food is better for both you and the planet. Not using chemicals on your fruit and vegetables supports bees, protects the good bugs and other animals, and it actually tastes better!

Two of the best ways you can fertilize your garden without using chemicals are:

- Using worm juice from a worm farm.
- Using compost instead of fertilizer.

DID YOU KNOW?

Once upon a time, all food was organic. It was only after World War II that chemical insecticides and fertilizers were introduced. Some of these chemicals were discovered by scientists during the war: they found that the same chemical used as nerve gas could also kill insects. Before then, food wasn't "organic," it was just food.

INSECT REPELLENTS

Instead of using herbicides and pesticides on your garden, try the two simple homemade options outlined here. When you spray your plants, remember you're aiming to keep hungry little insects away, not kill them. Your garden is a wonderful mini-ecosystem full of good microbes and fungi as well as good insects (like ladybugs, praying mantises, hoverflies, and lacewings) that eat the bad insects. You don't want to harm your little ecosystem.

ACTIVITY

SOAP SPRAY

What to do:

1. Add one tablespoon of soap flakes to two cups of water. Stir until dissolved.

2. Add to spray bottle and spray affected plants.

GARLIC SPRAY

ACTIVITY

What to do:

1. Puree two whole bulbs of garlic in a blender.

2. Cover with warm, soapy water and allow to soak overnight.

3. Strain the liquid into one quart of water, then add to spray bottle and spray affected plants.

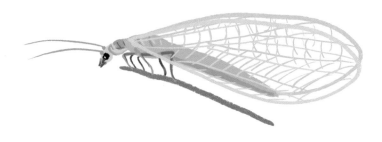

DID YOU KNOW?

You can also look into companion planting as another pesticide-free way to keep bugs away. This means putting plants together that help each other out. For example, planting garlic, chives, or spring onions near your flowers and other vegetables can keep away certain bugs. Growing anise with your vegetables will also keep away aphids.

TIP

Plant mint, fennel, dill, sunflowers, and dandelions to attract good bugs to your garden.

SLOW FOOD USA

The mission of Slow Food USA is to "reconnect Americans with the people, traditions, plants, animals, fertile soils, and waters that produce our food." One of the main ways they do that is through their school garden program, which gives kids hands-on experience with growing, harvesting, preparing, and enjoying their very own healthy food. Slow Food USA also hosts gatherings and provides all kinds of resources to educators, families, and communities. Check to see if there's a garden near you!

What are some tips for kids who want to cook their own delicious food?

1. **Get seasonal:** Find out which veggies, fruits, and herbs are in season in your area—they will be fresh and cheap at the market. Growing your own veggies, fruits, and herbs in your garden (or in pots if you don't have much space) is a great way to learn what's in season.

2. **Experiment:** Get creative with your cooking and have fun discovering new tastes, textures, and smells. Create a "salad of the imagination" by combining different lettuces and fresh herbs with seasonal veggies and fruit, like summer sweet tomatoes, earthy autumn pumpkins, crunchy snow peas in winter, or vibrant spring broad beans. Finish it off with a dressing made with olive oil, lemon juice, and a sprinkle of salt—make it to your taste!

3. **Share:** Bring your family and friends together to share your kitchen creations. Be proud of what you've achieved, and sit together at a table with your loved ones to share the food you have made.

BEES ARE AMAZING—they are some of the hardest working creatures on the planet! If they didn't exist, the world would be in big trouble. We need bees to pollinate our native species and increase biodiversity.

Bees also play an important role in pollinating all sorts of fruits and vegetables, as well as crops that we use to feed livestock. But sadly, native bee populations are under threat. Their natural habitats are being lost to urban developments that don't have enough trees and flowers to keep the bees alive. They are also disappearing due to pesticide use and disease.

One in every three bites of food that we eat comes from plants that are pollinated by bees.

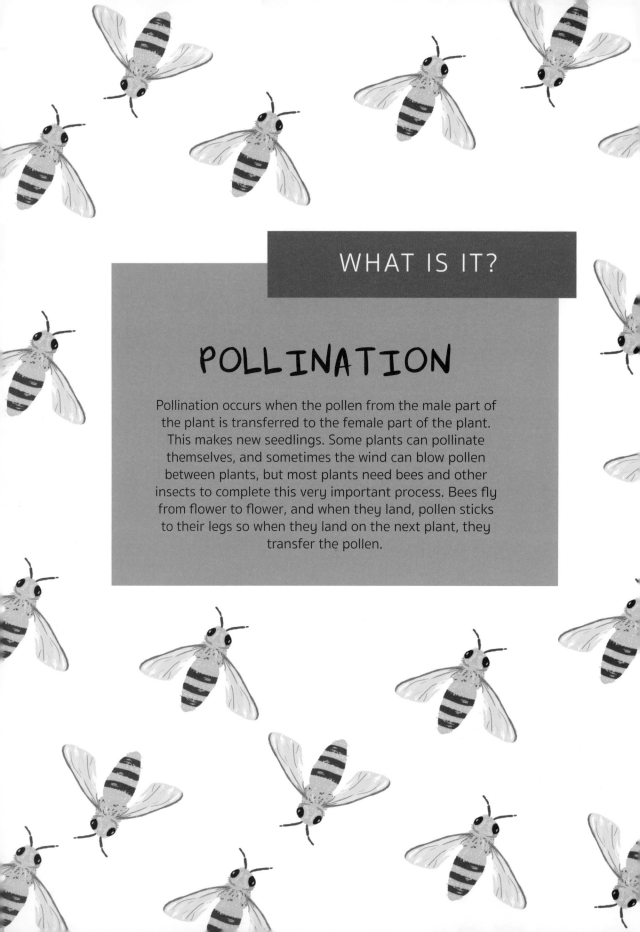

WHAT IS IT?

POLLINATION

Pollination occurs when the pollen from the male part of the plant is transferred to the female part of the plant. This makes new seedlings. Some plants can pollinate themselves, and sometimes the wind can blow pollen between plants, but most plants need bees and other insects to complete this very important process. Bees fly from flower to flower, and when they land, pollen sticks to their legs so when they land on the next plant, they transfer the pollen.

We can help bees by growing bee-friendly plants in our area. Bee-friendly plants include:

- **Flowers:** lavender, daisies, marigolds, roses, foxgloves, nasturtium, geraniums, clover, and sunflowers.
- **Herbs:** rosemary, basil, mint, thyme, parsley, fennel, cilantro, oregano, and sage.
- **Citrus trees:** lemon, lime, orange, and mandarin.
- **Trees:** bottlebrush, wattle, native flowering gums, tea tree, grevillea, jacaranda, lemon-scented myrtle, crab apple.
- **Berries:** strawberries, raspberries, and blueberries.

We can also support bee farmers by buying local, organic, fair-trade honey.

DID YOU KNOW?

The most bee-friendly
flowers are usually yellow,
blue, and purple.

MIKAILA ULMER
United States of America

When she was four years old, Mikaila had to come up with a product idea for a children's business competition. While she was thinking, she got stung by two bees in two weeks! Bee stings are not fun. Suddenly, Mikaila became fascinated with bees. She learned all about how they help our planet, and she wanted to do something to help them in return.

Around the same time, Mikaila's great-granny Helen sent the family a special recipe for flaxseed lemonade from a 1940s cookbook. Using this recipe, Mikaila later started a lemonade stand, using local honey to sweeten her lemonade and donating a percentage of the profits to local and international organizations that help protect bees.

Now Mikaila is thirteen years old and the CEO of Me & the Bees Lemonade. Her slogan is "Buy a Bottle, Save a Bee." She is one of the youngest business owners in the United States, and her lemonade is stocked in more than five hundred stores. In 2015, former US President Barack Obama even invited Mikaila to the White House so he could try her lemonade.

Even though she runs her own company, Mikaila still manages to make time for her school work. And it all started with her little lemonade stand, where she squeezed all the lemons herself. She's certainly a busy bee!

A BUTTERFLY GARDEN

WHO DOESN'T LOVE butterflies? They grow from an egg into a caterpillar, hop into a cocoon, and when they come out they can fly. But butterflies do more than just look pretty—they actually help pollinate flowers and plants, just like bees. As caterpillars, they stop plant species from getting out of control, and they are both predator and prey.

Butterflies are extremely sensitive to changes in their environment, so scientists track them to make sure an ecosystem is healthy. They also study the population numbers to evaluate the effects of environmental issues like climate change.

Pesticides, urbanization, and climate change all threaten the sensitive butterfly. Here are some ways for you to help butterflies and draw them to your area.

DID YOU KNOW?

There are around twenty thousand species of butterfly in the world. The US is home to more than seven hundred of these.

— HOW TO — ATTRACT BUTTERFLIES

1. Avoid using any pesticides or herbicides.

2. Find out what species of butterfly are native to your area, and then research what their caterpillars look like and what they eat—caterpillars can be fussy eaters! Plant these caterpillar-friendly plants in your garden, and don't worry if some of them get nibbled on: just remember that you are helping the butterflies.

3. Choose a sunny spot—butterflies don't like to stay in the shade too long—and plant nectar–rich flowers and plants such as marigolds, verbena, heliotrope, alyssum, daisies, wattle, banksia, bottlebrush, and eucalyptus. Butterflies love bright colors, so make sure you have lots of colorful flowers, especially pink, white, and red.

4. Butterflies love overgrown plants, so don't worry about taming your garden.

5. Butterflies like to mud-puddle, meaning they will sit in mud and suck the moisture out. Place a shallow dish of muddy water in a sunny spot.

ENERGY, ELECTRICITY, AND WATER

WE OFTEN TAKE electricity and water for granted—it can be easy to forget that we're lucky to have access to these things. This means many of us don't really consider how much energy we use and what impact that has. Energy production causes toxic fumes and greenhouse gases, and most forms of electricity production use up Earth's natural resources, such as trees, coal, and natural gas. Using less energy helps save these limited resources. There is also a limited supply of drinking water on the planet, so we should all learn to use water carefully and responsibly. And reducing our water usage in general helps reduce the energy needed to deliver it to us.

The less energy we use, the better!

Saving energy and water starts at home. With a few simple changes, you can help make the planet healthier and look after its future.

USING LESS ELECTRICITY

THERE ARE MANY simple ways you can reduce your electricity use, which will be good for both the planet and your parents' electricity bill!

TURN OFF THE LIGHTS
Every time you leave a room, make sure to turn the light off behind you. (But if someone shouts "Hey!," you might need to turn it back on again.)

START UNPLUGGING
Did you know that when things are plugged in to outlets, they still use energy—even if they're not switched on? Install outlet shut-off switches if possible, and unplug appliances like your toaster and kettle when they aren't being used. Unplug phone chargers when they're not in use. Turn off the TV when no one's watching it, and don't leave computers and consoles on overnight or when you're going outside to play.

What are you waiting for? Start unplugging today!

DOING THE LAUNDRY

Sunshine is a magical thing. As well as being a wonderful natural resource, sunlight can also disinfect your clothes, because the UV light damages bacteria. So instead of wasting electricity using the clothes drier, hang your clothes outdoors to dry.

When washing your clothes, it's also best to use cold water as often as possible. Heating up the water to do laundry is one of the biggest sources of energy use in the average home.

HEATING AND COOLING

If you can, try to avoid using the air conditioner or heater when possible. The energy used to run heating and cooling is the most expensive contributor to the average energy bill, making up almost half of the cost.

SOLAR POWER

We depend on the Sun for a lot—without it, there would be no life on Earth. The Sun produces energy that never runs out. With the help of solar panels, we can capture the Sun's energy, meaning we don't have to use Earth's precious resources to generate power. Encourage your parents, school, and local businesses to look into getting solar panels installed.

POWERSHOP

Powershop is an Australian energy company that sells electricity and gas, and they are the only energy retailer in the country that's 100% carbon neutral. Carbon is a greenhouse gas that is emitted when people use energy; Powershop supports environmental projects, like tree planting, to reverse the damage caused by the carbon. Powershop was also ranked Australia's greenest power company by Greenpeace in 2014, 2015, and 2018. By helping people reduce their energy usage, they're working to make a better future for our planet.

What are your top tips for kids who want to cut down their energy use?

1. Read a book in the sunshine instead of watching TV inside.

2. Don't be scared of the dark; you can see the stars better when the lights are off.

3. Put on a hoodie and cuddle your cat or dog or bunny or guinea pig instead of turning the heater on.

4. If you have the heater or air conditioner on, keep the doors and windows closed tight!

5. Don't open and close the fridge all the time (unfortunately, it doesn't make yummy food appear, but it does waste energy).

FINN VICARS
Australia

Finn Vicars is passionate about science, renewable energy, and inventing! He wants to use science to create a better future for our planet and help kids become greener and more sustainable. And he even met the prime minister of Australia!

1. How old are you now, and how old were you when you became interested in renewable energy?

I'm ten right now. When I became really passionate about renewables, I was about seven.

2. Where did you grow up and how did that inspire you?

I've lived in a lot of places. Until I was two and a half, I grew up in Melbourne but I don't remember much about it. Then I was in Sydney until I was about six or seven, and now I live on some acres on the Mid North Coast. It's been an amazing experience moving from a small rented apartment with the beach only a four-minute walk away to being on twenty-four acres with lots of space. We have our own section of river and it's pretty amazing.

3. What's your favorite subject at school and why?

Science is my favorite subject hands down! I'm in fifth grade but I do ninth-grade science. It's my passion in every way. I can't say why, but I suppose it extends from just wanting to understand how things work.

4. What do you want to be when you're older?

I'd like to be an astrophysicist, a quantum physicist, and an entrepreneur; I like inventing things!

5. Why are solar panels important?

Solar panels—and all other forms of renewable energy, like geothermal energy and wind energy, among others—allow us to produce our much-craved electricity in a way that doesn't harm our environment. Climate change caused by burning fossil fuels and low-efficiency products using electricity, like incandescent bulbs—everyone should replace them immediately!—is a big problem. A VERY big problem.

6. Tell us about the Living Off the Land Act that you presented to the former Australian prime minister Malcom Turnbull.

It was draft legislation—a suggested new law—to help make Australia a cleaner place. I wanted the government to make every Australian reduce their carbon footprint by using more renewables, more water from roof-water harvesting, eating more sustainably grown food, and recycling more.

7. What is your biggest achievement so far?

Probably going to meet the prime minister. It was amazing.

8. Do you have any tips for kids who want to reduce their carbon footprint?

Have you ever realized the power of nagging your parents? You need to tap your parents on the shoulder: we've got to get solar panels. We've got to get roof-harvested water for our garden. Even a small tank will help. Kids have a lot more power than they think.

DID YOU KNOW?

Along with the Sun, electricity can also be made from wind, water, and even animal manure.

SAVING WATER

WATER IS ESSENTIAL to life on Earth. Even though most of Earth is covered in water, only a very small percentage of this is available for drinking. It also takes a lot of energy to process and deliver water to your home. We all need to do our best to conserve this precious resource.

Here are some easy ways you can start saving water.

TAKE SHORTER SHOWERS

Did you know that reducing your daily shower time by just one minute can save over nine hundred gallons of water a year? Try using a timer to make sure you're not spending too long in the shower.

USE A SHOWER BUCKET

Putting a bucket in your shower means that instead of all the water going down the drain, you can save it. That water can then be used to water your plants. If you have a bath, you could reuse that water for your garden too.

TURN OFF THE FAUCET

Leaving the tap running can waste a huge amount of water! While you're brushing your teeth, make sure you turn off the water. When you're doing the dishes, turn off the faucet in between rinsing items.

THE DISHWASHER

Dishwashers use around three-and-a-half gallons of water per load, so only put the dishwasher on when it's full.

REUSE YOUR TOWEL

You can use a towel a few times before it needs to be washed—just hang it up to dry after each use.

SPOT THE LEAKS

Be a leak detective. Can you spot any leaky faucets in your house? Make sure you let your parents know!

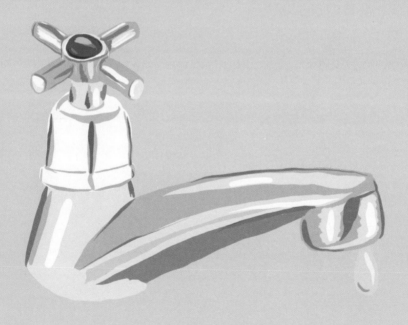

KELVIN DOE
Sierra Leone

Kelvin Doe grew up with his mother and four older siblings in a poor area of Freetown, the capital city of Sierra Leone, Africa. There were often cuts to the power, and the lights would only come on once a week. Kelvin knew he had to work out a way to fix this problem. He was determined to help his family and his community, but he didn't have access to many resources.

When he was ten years old, he began collecting electronic parts from dump sites and taking them apart to see how they worked. Using the things he found, Kelvin became a self-taught engineer, making a battery to power the lights in his home and other homes in his neighborhood, as well as making his own FM radio transmitter. Kelvin eventually started his own radio station. In his community he was called DJ Focus, because he believes that if you focus, you can create an invention perfectly. People loved his radio station—he provided them with news and music, and his listeners would send in texts, which he would read out.

Then one day, Kelvin won an award for a generator that he'd built using scrap metals, and was invited to be a guest resident at the Massachusetts Institute of Technology in the United States for three weeks. Kelvin was the youngest person ever to receive this invitation. Kelvin had never left his home in Sierra Leone before, and he missed his family, especially his mother, and the food in his country.

Now Kelvin is twenty-two years old and one of the world's most respected young African inventors. In 2017, he was named one of the 100 Most Influential Young Africans in the Africa Youth Awards. He runs his own company, KDoe-Tech Inc., and also founded the Kelvin Doe Foundation.

ANIMAL ACTIVISM

WHETHER THEY ARE our pets or they live in the wild, animals can be cute, funny, beautiful, strange, mysterious, and magnificent. And we share the Earth with them—it is their home as much as ours.

Animals are what make our planet so special, and without them the world would be a much sadder, lonelier place.

It's important to protect the world's animals and make sure they're treated well. Every animal has its own life to live and its own internal, emotional world, and even if we can't always understand that, we can respect it.

Unfortunately, the biggest threats to animals come from humans, which means that it's up to us to help them. From pets in our homes to animals on farms to wild animals in faraway countries, all animals on Earth need our protection. There are lots of ways you can help keep our animals safe.

VOLUNTEER

A LOT OF PEOPLE who work with animals don't do it for the money—they do it because they love animals. These incredible people look after animals when they are under threat from injury, disease, or homelessness—or hunting, poaching, and other human activities such as land clearing, deforestation, and urban development. You could start by volunteering at your local animal shelter, and one day you might even have the opportunity to volunteer overseas, working with animals like elephants, rhinos, orangutans, and turtles.

FACT	In the United States, between six and eight million cats and dogs enter animal shelters every year.

IF YOUR FAMILY is looking to get a new pet, instead of going to a store or a breeder, adopt one from a shelter. Every year, millions of animals are put down—in other words, humanely killed—because they don't have homes, so by adopting one of these animals, you're saving its life.

By choosing not to buy from pet stores, you are refusing to support puppy farms.

While puppies in pet stores are cute, all across America there are puppy farms (sometimes called puppy factories or mills), which are essentially breeding machines, making puppies to sell for money. The puppies in these factories tend to live in very poor conditions, often filthy and overcrowded, and they don't get the proper care or medical attention they need.

Buying a pet is a big decision and a huge commitment, both of time and money. Animals need a lot of care and love every single day—they need to be trained, fed, bathed, given exercise, and taken to the vet regularly. So before you buy a pet, make sure it's the right choice for you.

SPEAK UP FOR ANIMALS

ANIMALS HAVE A language all of their own. Unfortunately, that means when animals are hurt, they can't tell us.

We have to be the voices for animals who can't ask for help when they need it. If you see animal abuse, report it. If you see an injured animal, don't just leave it; take it to a wildlife rehabilitator or veterinarian.

Different animals have different needs, but most wildlife rescue organizations recommend these three steps:

1. If you have found a sick, injured, or orphaned animal, remove any threat to the animal. This includes keeping all people and pets away to minimize stress to the animal until vet transport or a rescuer arrives.

2. If it is safe to do so, contain the animal in a warm, dark, quiet place. For example, gently wrap the animal in a towel and place it in a ventilated box with a lid, then transport it carefully to the nearest vet or wait for a rescuer to arrive.

3. Do not give the animal any food or water, unless instructed to by a vet or wildlife rescue professional.

Keep the phone number of your local wildlife rescue group handy in case you find an injured native animal. When you take an injured animal to the vet, call your local rescue group and let them know where you've taken the animal, so they can contact the vet.

HANDY
— NUMBERS —

Animal welfare services vary greatly from state to state. You might consider looking up which organizations are in your area. The website for Humane Society of the United States has a helpful directory for looking up wildlife rehabilitators around the country, but you may also want to find contact information for your local:

- Veterinarians.
- Animal shelters.
- State department of conservation or department of fish and wildlife.
- Animal nonprofit organizations.

Another way you can speak up for animals is to write a letter to the Department of Agriculture, your state/territory agriculture minister, your local representative, or a newspaper, expressing your concerns about the treatment of animals.

You can also raise awareness at your local supermarket and shops by encouraging them to stock animal-friendly products.

And importantly, you can spread the word among your friends, family, teachers, and classmates simply by starting conversations with them and encouraging everyone to be more aware of their choices, the impact those choices have, and how they can make a difference. Remember to use positive encouragement—this means explaining why these changes are good for animals, rather than focusing on why what people are doing is bad.

BUY CRUELTY FREE

ALWAYS **CHOOSE PRODUCTS** that are cruelty-free. This means not buying foods that were produced using inhumane practices. Make sure your meat is coming from a good place, where the animals lived in good conditions, and that the chickens who laid your eggs are being treated well.

When buying cosmetics, choose those that use natural ingredients and aren't tested on animals. It can be difficult to know if a product is cruelty-free just from looking at the packaging, so try to research the products you are buying and the company that makes them.

TIP

When growing your own food, don't use pesticides. Aside from the fact that bugs and insects are living creatures too, pesticides are also very harmful to ecosystems, as many other animals rely on insects as a food source. Exposure to the chemicals in pesticides can also be linked to things like cancer, kidney and liver damage, and birth defects in a number of different species. Some pesticides even do damage to birds' singing ability, which leaves them unable to find a mate.

—— SAY NO ——
TO PALM OIL

It's very difficult to avoid palm oil, as it is found in almost half of all household products, including baked goods, candies, shampoo, soaps, makeup, cleaning products, and toothpaste. It can be listed under many different names in the ingredients, making it tricky to know if the products you are using contain palm oil.

Ninety percent of palm oil comes from Indonesia and Malaysia. Palm oil is taken from a type of palm tree, and the way these trees are farmed destroys the rainforest habitats of orangutans. Demand for palm oil has grown so quickly that orangutans are being left with nowhere to live and are now considered a critically endangered species. Orangutans are majestic, nomadic creatures who share ninety-eight percent of our DNA. We need to do something before we lose them forever.

By avoiding palm oil, you help reduce the demand for it, which slows down the destruction of the orangutans' homes.

These are some of the alternative names for palm oil:

- Anything with the word "palm" in it.
- Cetyl alcohol.
- Cetyl palmitate.
- Elaeis guineensis.
- Emulsifiers 422, 430-36, 470-8, 481-3, 493-5.
- Glyceryl stearate.
- Octyl palmitate.
- Palm fruit oil.
- Palm kernel oil.
- Palm stearine.
- Palmate/palmitate.
- Palmitic acid.
- Palmityl alcohol.
- Palmolein.
- Sodium dodecyl sulfate.
- Sodium kernelate.
- Sodium laureth/lauryl sulphate.
- Sodium lauryl lactylate.
- Sodium lauryl sulfoacetate.
- Stearate.
- Steareth 2 & 20.
- Stearic acid.
- Vegetable glycerin.
- Vegetable oil.
- Vitamin A palmitate.

Keep this list handy and, when you shop, check the labels. Avoid buying products that contain any of these ingredients.

TIP

Palm sugar and vegetable gum are safe and do not contain palm oil. To be sure, you can find lists of palm oil-free products online.

If you see vegetable oil in food ingredients, check to see if the product is high in saturated fat. If it is, it probably contains palm oil, unless the product also contains coconut oil.

EAT FEWER ANIMAL PRODUCTS

THE SIMPLE ACT of shopping for food is actually one of the most powerful ways you can fight animal cruelty. Start by reducing the amount of meat, eggs, and dairy products you eat. Eat with compassion, which means choosing the meat carefully and making sure it has come from a good place where the animals were treated well.

Here are some tips for making positive changes to your diet:

- Make the changes slowly. Experiment with being a vegetarian one or two days a week and see how it goes.
- Work out which vegetables you like the most and make them the star of your meal.
- Think about the milk you're drinking. Did you know that cows only produce milk once they have given birth to a calf? This means that their newborn calves have to be taken away so the mother's milk can be collected. Consider drinking other kinds of milk, such as soy, rice, and almond or other nut milks. Just make sure these other milks have added calcium to ensure you have healthy bones.
- If your school has a cafeteria, encourage them to provide more meat-free options, and to avoid factory-farmed egg and meat products. Get your friends and family on board too.
- Remember to keep an open mind about all the different foods you can try.

If you decide to eat less meat and dairy, chat with your parents first. It's important to eat more foods that contain vitamin D, calcium, protein, iron, and omega-3 fatty acids. If you're cutting out animal products, you may also need to take vitamin B12 supplements. Here are some other foods you could eat more of to ensure you get the nutrition you need:

Vitamin D ---------------- Mushrooms and almond milk with added vitamin D. Get a little sunlight.

Calcium ------------------- Calcium-set tofu; sesame seeds; dried fruit; fortified foods like soy and almond milk; almonds; greens like kale, bok choy, and broccoli.

Protein ------------------- Beans, lentils, chickpeas, nuts, quinoa, chia seeds, tofu, oats, wild rice, soy milk.

Iron ----------------------- Lentils, tofu, quinoa, brown rice, oatmeal, pumpkin, cashew nuts, spinach, prune juice.

Omega-3 ---------------- Chia seeds, hemp seeds, kidney beans, brussels sprouts, walnuts, seaweed, blueberries, wild rice.

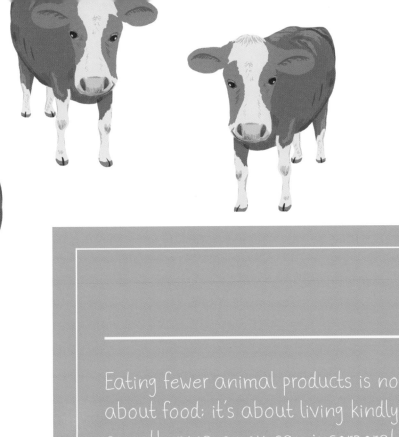

TIP

Eating fewer animal products is not just about food; it's about living kindly. There are other ways you can incorporate positive changes into your life, such as avoiding products tested on animals and not buying products that come from animals, such as leather, fur, and wool.

VOICELESS

Voiceless—the animal protection institute—was founded by father–daughter duo Brian and Ondine Sherman. The passionate team at Voiceless works to educate and inspire young people on how to protect animals, and they provide teachers with information and tools to teach students about the importance of relationships between humans and animals. They also run a program for law schools to teach about animal protection issues in our legal systems to try to inspire positive change.

What are your top tips for kids who want to do more to help animals?

1. Voiceless recommends slowly introducing a healthy plant-based lifestyle. Changing your daily diet has a direct effect on the lives of our most vulnerable and mistreated animals. And there are so many delicious and nutritious options!

2. Volunteer at a local animal shelter or sanctuary. Many animals, from dogs and hens to pigs, have gone through trauma or abandonment and your time and care can help them heal and make them feel loved.

3. Get active for animals by joining protests against cruelty and signing petitions. You can even write a letter to your local representative on an issue you care about. Every person, no matter their age, and every single voice can make a difference.

4. Organize a fundraising event for your favorite animal charity: a veggie sausage sizzle, fun run, or even a lemonade stand. It's also a great way to talk to others about the issues you care about.

GENESIS BUTLER
United States of America

When Genesis Butler was three years old, her favorite food was chicken nuggets. But when she found out from her mom where chicken nuggets came from, she stopped eating meat. When she was six, she asked her mom where milk came from. When she found out that it was the milk cows made for their babies, she made the decision to go vegan. She soon encouraged her family to join her.

By being vegan, Genesis knows she is helping both animals and the planet. At ten years old, she did her first TEDx talk on the connection between the environment and eating animals, and how being vegan can help heal the planet. Genesis has won many awards for her activism, including the Animal Hero Kids' Sir Paul McCartney Young Veg Advocate award, the Vegan Kid of the Year award, and PETA's Youth Activist of the Year.

She is now eleven years old and has started her own nonprofit foundation called Genesis for Animals, where she helps provide funding to animal sanctuaries and rescue groups. Through her foundation, she wants to save as many animals' lives as possible.

Even though she is actively involved in the animal rights movement, Genesis still finds time to be a kid. She loves playing football, singing, dancing, sewing, drawing, and spending time with her friends.

VEGETARIAN COOKING

These sausage rolls can be easily made vegan by using pastry made with oil instead of butter and leaving out the egg in the filling. Just note that without the egg to bind your ingredients, your filling will be a little crumblier.

RECIPE

VEGETARIAN SAUSAGE ROLLS

You'll need:

- ½ cup dry lentils.
- 2 cups vegetable stock.
- 2 tablespoons olive oil.
- 1 onion, finely chopped.
- 1 carrot, grated.
- 2 sticks celery, grated.
- 2 cloves garlic, minced.
- 2 tablespoons wholegrain mustard.
- 3 tablespoons freshly chopped parsley.
- 1 cup breadcrumbs.
- Salt and pepper, to season.
- 2 eggs (optional).
- 3 sheets frozen puff pastry.
- Sesame seeds (optional).

RECIPE

What to do:

1. Preheat oven to 390°F.

2. To cook the lentils, place them in a saucepan with the vegetable stock and bring to a boil. Then turn the temperature to low and allow to simmer for twenty to thirty minutes, or until the lentils are soft. Drain and set aside to cool.

3. Heat the olive oil in a large frying pan over medium heat, then add the onion, carrot, celery, and garlic. Cook until onion is golden. Add the mustard, cook for a further two minutes, and then set aside to cool.

4. In a large bowl, combine your cooked lentils, fried onion mixture, parsley, and breadcrumbs. Add salt and pepper to taste. Add eggs and mix until all ingredients are combined.

5. Cut your squares of puff pastry in half and then lay your filling down the long edge of each half. Fold the pastry over into a roll shape and join the edges, then cut into four even pieces. Repeat until you have used all the filling.

6. Put the rolls on a baking sheet and prick the tops with a fork. If adding sesame seeds, brush the tops of your rolls with a tiny amount of water first to make the seeds stick. Bake for fifteen to twenty minutes, or until pastry is golden.

NATIONAL PARKS
— AND NATURE —
RESERVES

National parks and nature reserves are designed to protect and conserve the unique animals and ecosystems within them, as well as places of cultural significance to Indigenous peoples. They are made up of untouched land and are incredibly beautiful, with diverse environments from rainforests to beaches, rock formations, caves, and deserts.

When you visit a national park, be sure not to litter or leave anything behind, and make sure you stay on the marked paths. Many plant species are very delicate and don't like to be disturbed. It's also important not to feed native wildlife, as their bodies are not designed to eat human food and it can make them sick.

You can also look into volunteering at a national park—people are always needed to help reduce certain kinds of weeds. You could also make a donation to support a conservation program.

Kids and family events are held in some national parks to raise awareness about why our national parks are so important and how they help protect our wildlife.

— SAY NO —
TO USING
ANIMALS FOR
ENTERTAINMENT

Don't support places where animals are used for entertainment—like animal racing, circuses, marine parks, and zoos, where animals are kept in very confined spaces or subjected to such rigorous training routines that they're often stressed. Animals should be able to live freely in their natural habitats, and not used for our amusement. Instead, choose a family outing that's kind to animals.

SOLLI RAPHAEL
Australia

Solli Raphael is a writer and award-winning slam poet who is inspiring young people everywhere to take action and fight for social equality, the environment, and animal protection. With his writing, he hopes to tackle all kinds of social issues, big and small.

1. How old are you now, and how old were you when you started writing and performing poetry?

I just had my fourteenth birthday. I write poetry and other genres of writing, but I guess I started writing when I was about seven years old. I remember writing comics, which would sometimes have rhyming sections. I used to write in all of my spare time, which kind of hasn't changed, so on the weekends, during the holidays, and even in the car on trips to my tennis tournaments. I started reading poetry from a really young age, and had my mom read it to me, but I really got into writing poetry when I was about ten. I started performing my slam poetry on stage when I was twelve.

2. Where did you grow up and how did that inspire you?

I grew up in a beachside country town of about 75,000 people, and literally the beach, the farming country, and the native bushlands are all in the region, with my home being between the Pacific Ocean and the Great Dividing Range on the North Coast of New South Wales. After school when I was in elementary school, I would play in the outdoors or help my mom in our organic veggie gardens. So I think this type of connection to nature has inspired me to be such a passionate poet, as I always seem to write about environmental protection. I have also seen firsthand what happens when people don't appreciate or look after the land properly, whether it's logging/deforestation in our local area, or commercial farms polluting waterways with overusing pesticides, or councils who remove one hundred-year-old trees just for redevelopment of an area but leave zero shade, or even people who litter as they're walking or from their cars—and animals that consume the litter or plastic who then die from it. I've seen that sort of thing too many times, and it's just frustrating and I think it's so avoidable. Inspiration is everywhere for me.

3. What is your favorite pastime or hobby?

I can never seem to pick a favorite, but I love going to the beach—and I enjoy reading and working on my poetry, books, and entrepreneurial projects.

4. What is the biggest inspiration for your poetry?

Sometimes, although I know it can be sensationalized, the news can inspire me. Seeing what is going on around the world often makes me angry or feel devastated, so those emotions usually lead me to writing a poem. The fact is that every single day, we have two choices: to make a positive or a negative change. And this is so empowering that I want others to realize that the entire future of everything is in our hands. The news just gives us one side, so I find that I spend a lot of time on researching facts, which I enjoy doing too.

5. What is your biggest achievement so far?

It would be either having my own book, *Limelight*, published internationally, or performing one of my poems in front of a live audience of 35,000 people at the 2018 Gold Coast Commonwealth Games—that was FUN! Or, the time I delivered a TEDx talk—that was probably the hardest achievement. Being the youngest ever winner of the Australian Poetry Slam was also a great experience. Sorry—hard to pick one because there've been some really great opportunities.

6. Do you have any advice for how other young people can start making a difference in the world?

YES! It's easier than you think. You just have to figure out what you want to do to make a change, and do it. As I've always loved writing, I guess I have learned to use this to help express my thoughts. If someone isn't sure how they can make a difference in the world, here's a few of my tips:

— Find what you are passionate about or inspired by, and find ways to connect with it—my TEDx talk was on this exact topic!

— Find others who inspire you, and follow them on social media or watch their YouTubes. Learn from the people who have found their way in what they like to do to help greater causes, which are causes that are bigger than their own needs.

— Focus on just one cause first, otherwise you might get overwhelmed with how many causes there are—there's so many!

7. **If you could change one thing about the world, what would it be?**
Governmental policies that would combat greed and poor environmental
choices, so that the planet could be repaired from climate change and
pollution—and so that the poor and vulnerable people around
the world could have a better life.

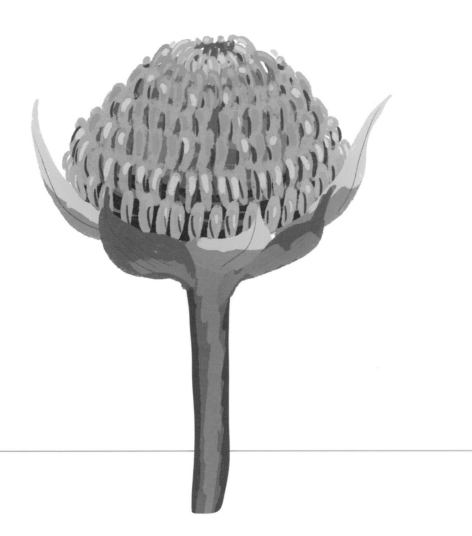

AN
ACT OF
KINDNESS

CHANGING THE WORLD doesn't only mean helping the planet and its plants and animals. It also means making a difference in the lives of the people around you. Choose to be kind to people, because sometimes the world can be unkind. Besides, being nice has been scientifically proven to be good for you too. Kindness boosts something in our bodies called serotonin, which makes us feel happier and more positive.

Sometimes it's difficult to be nice when you are feeling down, but it's always best to try. You might even start to feel better yourself—any act of kindness, no matter how big or small, helps your family, friends, the people around you, the environment, and the world.

The world can be a difficult place for many people, whether it's because they are elderly, sick, poor, homeless, lonely, unhappy, or just having a bad day.

HOW TO

BE NICE IN

EVERYDAY

WAYS

PRACTICE BEING nice in these simple ways every day:

- Smile at people. Smiling makes everyone feel better.
- Always say good morning.
- Listen when people are talking to you before responding. People enjoy talking about themselves!
- Give someone a compliment.
- Hold the door for someone.
- Offer your seat to someone on public transportation.
- Say hi to someone at school who you don't usually talk to.
- Try to understand how others are feeling. This is called empathy.
- If someone looks upset, ask if they are OK.
- Help people when they are struggling. If your mom or dad has lots to do, offer your support.
- Do a chore without being asked—and without telling anyone.
- Thank people when they do something nice for you.
- Make breakfast for your family, or help a friend or sibling with their homework.
- Remember to be kind to yourself too.

A KINDNESS JOURNAL

Start a journal and write down one nice thing you do each day. Kindness can actually take some practice!

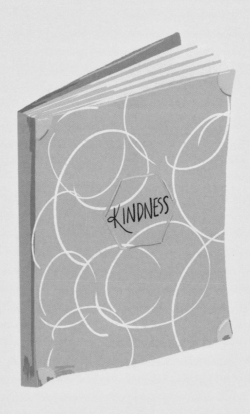

FORGIVE

Learn the power of forgiveness. When you are feeling hurt and angry, it can be hard to overcome those feelings. Make a conscious decision to let go of your grudge, your anger, or thoughts of revenge, and make amends—it is the best thing to do for everyone, but most of all, for yourself. Avoid dwelling on all the ways you thought the other person was wrong. Forgiving someone doesn't mean that you agree with what they did; it just means that you can move forward and leave it in the past.

Forgiveness has been shown to reduce stress and anxiety, make you happier, improve your self-esteem, and increase your positive emotions.

JAYLEN ARNOLD
United States of America

Jaylen Arnold is a public speaker, anti-bullying educator, and activist from Lakeland, Florida. When Jaylen was three years old, he was diagnosed with Tourette's Syndrome, which meant he had vocal and motor "tics." Tics aren't the bugs, Jaylen likes to say, they're movements and sounds you can't control— kind of like a sneeze. He would often let out verbal squeals for no apparent reason, which interrupted his daily living.

While his condition was sometimes challenging, school was much worse— Jaylen suffered constant bullying. Other kids would mock him and copy his tics, which only made the symptoms worse. After switching schools, Jaylen decided to take a stand.

> "The more we understand each other, the more we will love the differences we have and the similarities we share."

At the age of eight, he founded Jaylen's Challenge to promote the awareness and prevention of bullying through education and community service. With the help of a few adults, Jaylen created a website and started an official charitable organization. He soon realized he was far from alone in his struggles—so many others were being bullied around the globe on a daily basis, children and adults alike.

Jaylen came up with a motto, "Bullying, no way!" He then made glow-in-the dark wristbands with the intention of drawing attention to the issue. Within no time, Jaylen was being asked to speak at schools all around the country, and he was featured on Nickelodeon, CNN, ABC, NBC, CBS, Fox, and *The Ellen Show*. He got to meet and collaborate with all kinds of celebrities, and he became the only American ever to receive the Princess Diana Legacy Award from Prince William and Prince Harry.

Over the past decade, Jaylen's anti-bullying campaign has educated thousands and changed lives. While he's studying in college now, Jaylen is still working to educate the educators, teach tolerance to the tormentors, and banish bullying for all.

— SHARING — AND DONATING

If someone is in need or has less than you, share what you have—even if it's just your lunch. Donate the toys and clothes you no longer need to charities and thrift stores—just remember to only give things that are in good condition and can still be used. Thrift stores have to spend a lot of money every year trying to get rid of the things they can't sell.

RAISING

AWARENESS

THE MORE PEOPLE know about an issue, the better. Learn as much as you can about issues that are important to you. For example, maybe you are particularly passionate about some of the things you have read about in this book:

- Plastic pollution.
- Ethical fashion.
- Reducing waste.
- The meat, egg, and fishing industries.
- Organic food.
- Saving energy and water.
- Animal welfare.

Or maybe you feel strongly about some other important causes, such as:

- Youth homelessness.
- People affected by natural disasters like hurricanes, floods, and earthquakes.
- Refugees and asylum seekers.
- Kids' education.
- Cancer research and treatment.

Once you have informed yourself, educate your friends and family about the issue. You can start a petition online to raise awareness and make a change, or write a letter to a newspaper. Spread the word and help others learn about the issue too. Encourage discussion about the issue in your community. Do what you can to help the people involved in these causes.

RAISING MONEY

You can raise money for a good cause. Like Mikaila Ulmer, you too can set up a lemonade stand and donate the money you raise to a cause you feel strongly about. Or if you are good at something else, such as sewing, knitting, pottery, art, making jewelry, woodwork, or baking, you can sell the things you make to raise money.

Think about all the things you care about and write them down, then look into organizations that are fighting to help. On their websites, look for information about how to donate the money you raise and other ways you can become part of the solution.

ADELINE TIFFANIE SUWANA

Indonesia

Adeline Tiffanie Suwana lives in Indonesia. When she was young, she became worried about the natural disasters that were happening in her hometown. At twelve years old, she formed a community of young people like herself called Sahabat Alam, which means "Friends of Nature."

Together with her group, Adeline began planting mangrove trees and coral reefs, and she also helped with fish breeding and turtle protection. She then began tackling different environmental problems, organizing to clean up debris on coastal beaches and introducing green clubs in schools.

Through Sahabat Alam, Adeline also helped manage the Electric Generator Water Reel project to provide remote villages with electricity.

Adeline has been an inspiration to young people both in her community and around the world, creating a generation of kids who love nature and the environment and want to do something to protect it.

In 2009, she was presented with the Action for Nature International Young Eco-Hero award for her incredible work.

— ORGANIZATION —

FOOD RESCUE US

Food Rescue US is America's leading food rescue organization. Restaurants and other commercial food outlets have to obey strict food safety guidelines. Fresh food can only be kept for a few hours. Once it is cooked or displayed, if it isn't sold or eaten within a few hours, it has to be thrown out that same day. Food Rescue US organizes to collect any excess food that commercial outlets may have, in order to prevent the food being thrown in the garbage. They then deliver it to community kitchens and food pantries all around the country. Not only are they cutting down on food waste, they're also helping support people in need.

How can kids make a difference when it comes to food waste?

1. **Be a Food Fighter!** A third of all food goes to waste, which is just crazy when so many still go hungry. Make sure you don't waste your food; eat it all up, especially what's in your lunchbox!

2. **Love your food!** Take time to understand how food is grown and produced, how long it takes, and all the resources that are used. If you see an odd-looking carrot—buy it. If your apple has a bruise—eat it. Wasting food wastes everything, so be sure you don't throw it away.

3. **Be a change-maker!** There are so many ways you can make a difference, from ensuring your friends, family, or school don't waste food, to getting your hands dirty in the garden by growing your own food or getting a compost bin or worm farm going. The planet will thank you!

MAKE A CHRISTMAS JAR

Using a repurposed jar, collect all your small change throughout the year. During the holiday season, donate all the money in the jar to a charity of your choice. Put a label on your jar with the name of your chosen charity so you are reminded each day what you are fighting for.

There are many people with very little, and you can help give someone in need a better holiday. Creating the jar can be a fun project, and you can get your other family members to contribute too. Keep the jar in a central location in your home, so everyone can help.

Some charities you might choose to donate to include:
- The Salvation Army.
- Toys for Tots.
- The American Red Cross.
- Starlight Children's Foundation.
- Covenant House.
- United Way Worldwide.
- Oxfam.
- One Simple Wish.
- CARE USA.

DID YOU KNOW?

Louis Braille was only fifteen years old when he invented braille, a system of reading and writing for the blind or visually impaired.

GROUP ACTIVITIES

WE ALL NEED TO WORK TOGETHER

While it's important for us each to make changes in our own lives to help the world, it's also important for us to work alongside friends and family. So team up with friends who are eager to go on the mission to change the world with you. Some of the things you can do as a group are:

- Host a screening of an environmental documentary, and offer planet-friendly, plastic-free snacks. Some documentaries you might choose to show include:
  — *Life.*
  — *Planet Earth.*
  — *Blue Planet.*
  — *Living on One Dollar.*
  — *More Than Honey.*
  — *Hidden Kingdoms.*
  — *Arctic Tale.*
  — *Oceans.*
  — *The 11th Hour.*

- Organize a beach, park, or river cleanup.

- Go on a trash walk with your friends. Pick your local park, beach, nature reserve, or waterway. Take along a pair of gloves each and a bucket, and collect all the trash you can find to make your area a nicer place to live.

- Organize a lemonade stand to raise money for a charity you like.

- Ask your parents if you can carpool, cycle, or walk when you have to go somewhere.

- Start conversations. Awareness is the first step toward being able to make a change. Over dinner, talk about the things you have learned in this book, and encourage others to learn from you and start making changes.

RESOURCES

CHANGEMAKERS

Amy and Ella Meek

kidsagainstplastic.co.uk

facebook.com/kidsVplastic

Earth Bottles

earthbottles.com.au

instagram.com/earthbottles

Elif Bilgin

elif-bilgin.com

instagram.com/elifbilginofficial

Felix Finkbeiner

plant-for-the-planet.org/en/home

facebook.com/FFinkbeiner

Food Rescue US

foodrescue.us

facebook.com/FoodRescueUS

Genesis Butler

genesisforanimals.org

instagram.com/
   aveganchildsjourneygenesis

Good On You

goodonyou.eco

instagram.com/goodonyou_app

Greta Thunberg

fridaysforfuture.org

www.instagram.com/
   gretathunberg

twitter.com/GretaThunberg

Jaylen Arnold

jaylenschallenge.org

twitter.com/jayschallenge

youtube.com/user/
   jaylenschallenge

Josh Murray

joshsrainboweggs.com.au

instagram.com/joshsrainboweggs

Katie Stagliano

katieskrops.com

instagram.com/katieskrops

Kelvin Doe

twitter.com/Kelvinbdoe

Maya Penn

instagram.com/mayasideas

facebook.com/mayasideas

Mikaila Ulmer

meandthebees.com

instagram.com/mikailasbees

Milo Cress

www.ecocycle.org/bestrawfree

Powershop

powershop.com.au

Ruby the Climate Kid

facebook.com/TheClimateKid

twitter.com/theclimatekid

Slow Food USA

slowfoodusa.org

facebook.com/SlowFoodUSA

Solli Raphael

instagram.com/solli_raphael

facebook.com/solliraphael

Take 3 for the Sea

take3.org

instagram.com/take3forthesea

The Compost Revolution

compostrevolution.com.au

instagram.com/
  thecompostrevolution

Voiceless

voiceless.org.au

instagram.com/voiceless.org.au

ORGANIZATIONS

American Community Garden Association: communitygarden.org

American Society for the Prevention of Cruelty to Animals: aspca.org

Choose Cruelty Free: choosecrueltyfree.org

eXXpedition: exxpedition.com

Farmers Market Coalition: farmersmarketcoalition.org

Feeding America: feedingamerica.org

Greenpeace: greenpeace.org

Keep America Beautiful: kab.org

Leaping Bunny Program: leapingbunny.org

National Wildlife Federation: nwf.org

PETA: peta.org

Plastic Film Recycling: plasticfilmrecycling.org

Responsible Cafes: responsiblecafes.org

Seafood Watch: seafoodwatch.org

Sea Shepherd: seashepherd.org

Seasonal Food Guide: seasonalfoodguide.com

The Humane Society of the United States: humanesociety.org

The Orangutan Foundation International: orangutan.org

STORES

Azure Standard Bulk Foods: azurestandard.com

KeepCup: us.keepcup.com

Lush: lushusa.com

Who Gives A Crap: us.whogivesacrap.org

CHARITIES

American Cancer Society: cancer.org

CARE USA: care.org

Covenant House: covenanthouse.org

Ferst Readers: ferstreaders.org

One Simple Wish: onesimplewish.org

Oxfam: oxfam.org

Prevent Blindness: preventblindness.org

Red Cross: redcross.org

StandUp for Kids: standupforkids.org

Starlight Children's Foundation: starlight.org

St Vincent de Paul Society: svdpusa.org

The Salvation Army: salvationarmyusa.org/usn/brighten-the-holidays

Toys for Tots: toysfortots.org

UNICEF USA: unicefusa.org

United Way Worldwide: unitedway.org

PARKS

Canadian National Parks: pc.gc.ca/en/index

National Forest Foundation: nationalforests.org

National Park Foundation: nationalparks.org

The National Association of State Park Directors: stateparks.org

The Sierra Club: sierraclub.org

United States Forest Service: fs.usda.gov

US National Parks: nps.gov

ACKNOWLEDGMENTS

My journey to write this book is not one I went on alone.

My biggest thanks go to the wonderful team at Pantera Press, without whom this book would not exist. Ali, Marty, John, and Jenny, thank you for always believing in me and giving me new and exciting opportunities. Thanks to my publisher, Lex, for your wisdom and insight, and for reminding me to take off my editor hat once in a while and be an author. And thanks to the rest of my incredibly talented, dedicated, and passionate team: James, Anna, Katy, Anabel, Lucy, Anne, and Kirsty. Thanks also to my US publisher, Andrews McMeel, in particular to Kevin Kotur who has championed this book.

To Elly Clapin, design superstar, who turned my words into something beautiful.

And to Astred Hicks, whose illustrations and cover design make me smile every time I see them. You've brought my book to life.

To my editor, Vanessa Lanaway, for your thoughtful and considered feedback.

Thank you to James Searle, my composting and worm farm guru. You encouraged me to write this book and have been with me every step of the way. Thank you for everything.

Thank you to my parents, Francesca and Adrian, my biggest supporters, who have always been by my side, and to my family, Chip, Maddy, Jerry, and Olivia.

A huge thank-you to all the kids and organizations who made this book possible and inspired me with their passion: Milo Cress, Frieda and Felix Montefiore, Greta Thunberg, Josh Murray, Ruby Tarman, Finn Vicars, Solli Raphael, Jaylen Arnold, Amy and Ella Meek, Maya Penn, Elif Bilgin, Katie Stagliano, Felix Finkbeiner, Mikaila Ulmer, Kelvin Doe, Genesis Butler, Adeline Tiffanie Suwana, Earth Bottles, Good On You, Take 3 for the Sea, The Compost Revolution, Slow Food USA, Powershop, and Food Rescue US.

And lastly, a big thank-you to you, and all the other kids out there who want to make a difference. Let's change the world together.

ABOUT THE AUTHOR

Lucy Bell is a book editor and music teacher on a journey to live a more ethical, sustainable, and mindful life.

After getting her Bachelor of Arts degree at the University of Sydney with majors in English and Ancient History, Lucy studied a Master of Publishing. Now she works for a social-purpose publishing house making big differences and helping fund nonprofits and charities to close the literacy gap.

Lucy grew up on the New South Wales Central Coast of Australia surrounded by four siblings, a cat, two dogs, two sheep, a lizard, lots of guinea pigs, and thirteen chickens. She now lives in Sydney and, while watering her balcony garden, dreams of one day owning her own country farmhouse.

AUTHOR'S NOTE

The ideas in this book are just the beginning of your journey to help the world and save our planet.

It's now up to you.

Keep learning more about the difference you can make, and keep doing more to make sure those changes happen. There is always something else we can do. Be inspired to make changes, and inspire others to do the same.

You can do anything—even change the world.

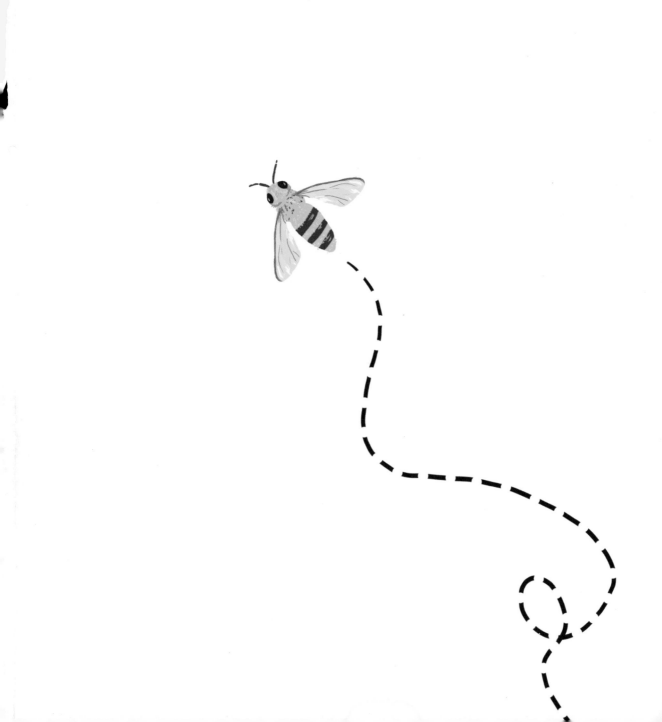